The One Thousand and First Night

A play by

Bahram Beyzaie

Translation and Critical Analysis by

Saeed Talajooy

Bisheh Publishing – San Francisco, USA

The One Thousand and First Night

A Play by Bahram Beyzaie

Translated by Saeed Talajooy

Written in : 2002
Translated in : 2011
Cover Design : Mohsen Valihi

Library of Congress Control Number : 2023930465
ISBN : 978-1-7355686-7-6

Bisheh Publishing – San Francisco, USA
Bisheh.publishing@gmail.com
www.bisheh-publishing.com
Published in the United States of America

Contents

Contents

A Note on Bahram Beyzaie and This Translation

Bahram Beyzaie (1938-) is the most prominent and versatile Iranian playwright of the last 60 years. He is also one of the country's greatest filmmakers and a leading scholar of Iranian folklore, mythology, dramatic rituals and performing traditions. In the course of his dramatic and cinematic career, Beyzaie has produced more than a hundred plays, screenplays and films, some of which are counted among the greatest masterpieces of Persian dramatic literature and Iranian cinema.

From his earliest plays, Beyzaie has displayed a preoccupation with marginalized forms, characters and events and has used his precision of vision and divergent ways of seeing and writing to highlight the cultural failures that have produced the dominant exclusionist discourses that have beleaguered life in Iran since the ancient times. His plays, therefore, often deal with myth, history and folklore, to reflect the continuity of the vicious methods of domination, the cultural failures that leave people at the mercy of internal tyrants and external exploiters and the significance of the positive sides of Iranian culture which have enabled it to survive.

This preoccupation with the historical and mythical identities of Iranian peoples and their personal and collective manifestations, failures and achievements turns his plays into loci of negotiation between the past and present where he uses the resources of Iran's folk tradition to write a history of the silenced peoples. It also creates a space for him in which he mythologizes the present

5

positive and destructive forces to show their links with their archetypal and historical origins and demythologizes the past to show the humanity of the sacred or evil figures in ways that subvert the forming narratives of contemporary dominant discourses. The same preoccupation has also provided him with a space to experiment with the stage language and reformulate Iranian indigenous performing traditions. In the case of language, in many of his works, he displays his unique mastery of different class, gender and profession registers of Persian in various historical eras without sinking into a stilted imitation of the literary, historical and religious texts of the past. He has, thus, produced highly performable pieces that have functioned as models of dramatic language for three generations of Iranian playwrights. In the case of indigenous forms, he has been the most influential person in the rise of modern indigenous-style Iranian drama both as a scholar and as a practitioner working with these forms in his plays and films.

The idea of translating *The One Thousand and First Night* occurred to me when I was writing my PhD thesis on a comparative study of Bahram Beyzaie and Wole Soyinka in 2006. The stylistic and linguistic variety and versatility of the play and its focus on some of Beyzaie's main themes and two of his main sources of inspiration, the *Shahnameh* and *One Thousand and One Night* make it unique and place it in par with his greatest plays and screenplays including *So Dies Akbar the Hero* (1963), *The Eighth Journey of Sinbad* (1965), *Death of Yazdgerd* (1979), *Kalât Claimed* (1982), *New Preface to the Shahnameh* (1986), *Parchment of Master Sharzin* (1986), *Reed Panel* (1992), *Account of Bondar the Premier* (1961-1995), and *Afrâ or the Day Is Passing* (1997). Its three-part structure and focus on the fate of a book and its emancipatory potential is also significant as it offers a new way of representing cultural continuity and the roles that creative women and men have played in it. I finally translated the play in 2010 and finalized it in 2011, but never found the time to do the final revision for publication.

The most difficult aspect of translating the play was Beyzaie's focus on the encounter of two languages and two cultures in the colonial context of the second part of the play, particularly the renaming scenes and the language of the new ruling elite which mixes Arabic and Persian in ways that distort the essence of the Persian language. The mixing of Persian and Arabic in that part remains untranslatable, but I conveyed the idea of renaming by using the English translations of the characters' names instead of Arabic ones. I have tried to remain as loyal to the original play as possible and to convey the linguistic games and figures of speech that Beyzaie uses in the poetic phrases and repartee scenes of the first and third parts. As a rule, however, I went for a simpler form when such a practice was likely to undermine the play's performability in English.

At its cultural and political levels, the play is easy to follow and a delight to perform, watch, or read. Beyzaie's works, however, always function at several levels of suggestiveness among which the archetypal and historical levels are the most difficult and fascinating. To help the reader understand these layers and the complicated, culture specific concepts and practices that they work with, I have also included an analytical article in the book. The article is by no means exhaustive about the forms and themes that Beyzaie works with, but it can be used as an introductory guideline for further studies.

I hope you enjoy the play.

Saeed Talajooy
24 March 2022.

The
One Thousand and First Night
1

Characters:

Shahrnâz [Raconteur/The Indian Game Keeper/
The Untouchable Old Woman]

Arnavâz [The Adviser/ The Chef/ The Indian
Game Keeper/ and His Wife]

Zahhâk

The Stage:

Zahhâk's inner court, draped with brocade curtains.
Towards the back, on the right, a wood bed with
fretwork legs of lions wrapped by snakes, draped by
a mosquito net. In the front, on the left, the throne
with falcon shaped legs and snakes-headed handles.
Arnavâz, who is wearing a golden mask, is lying
back on the throne humorously feigning snoring.
Shahrnâz approaches her like a ghost wearing a
silver mask.

Shahrnâz:	Awake Zahhâk; it is the night of your end!
Arnavâz:	*[Moving her head quickly to left and right to say no]* Zzz! Mmm! Zzzz! *[As if in pain]* Ouch! Oh, oh!
Shahrnâz:	You reigned for a thousand nights, Zahhâk; now is the one thousand and first night!

[On the bed in the background, Zahhâk jumps from a nightmare yelling; with his frightened cry Shahrnâz and Arnavâz drop their masks, step backward and swiftly run to different corners. Zahhâk comes forward, panting.]

Zahhâk:	Shahrnâz! Arnavâz! Is it you? Or am I asleep?
Shahrnâz:	We are not your dream, Zahhâk. You are your own dream and the cause of our dreamless sleeplessness!
Zahhâk:	*[Suspicious]* Why are you awake?

Arnavâz:	*[With a fake yawn]* We became sleepless due to a dream!
Zahhâk:	A dream?
Arnavâz:	*[Humorously]* Nothing to consider a thing. Leave it be. Take women's dreams to be the opposite of what will be.
Zahhâk:	*[Suspicious]* When did I fall asleep; and where were you?
Shahrnâz:	Don't worry! No one, even us, can come near you. Unless we've got used to your snakes' venom!
Arnavâz:	*[Mocking]* or they to our scent!
Zahhâk:	*[Feeling unsafe]* My snakes — intoxicated with your sweet scent? So that you can dupe them with flirting? No — you come near me only when I want it!
Shahrnâz:	We only come as close as it is safe. We're not fed up with our lives, Zahhâk. Your snakes are unruly!
Zahhâk:	How good is the name of fear! And how good that you don't know archery or throwing daggers!
Arnavâz:	*[Poses like an archer]* With what daggers or bows and arrows, Zahhâk?
Zahhâk:	How good that women are not taught lassoing and sword fighting; or I would have to worry for my life all the time! And how

good that all the affairs of this inner room pass behind these six bolted doors, where no one has access; and my elite bodyguards and palace sentries are all alert and attentive behind every door! Yet you did not tell a tale, or I would remember!

Shahrnâz: This time you fell asleep before hearing our tale, Zahhâk!

Zahhâk: I didn't hear your tale, or you didn't have a tale?

Shahrnâz: We wove ever newer tales every night, weaving words into words; but tonight, we have one unlike the others!

Zahhâk: *[Suspicious]* Unlike the others?

Shahrnâz: The tale came to the teeth and pushed through the lips; yet no ears were awake for hearing!

Arnavâz: *[Placing an imaginary crown on her head]* Tonight will not pass without a tale, Zahhâk!

Shahrnâz: You reigned for a thousand nights, how is that for a tale?

Zahhâk: *[Pleased]* Ha, ha — the tale of my kingship? Yah — sounds great. *[Rubbing his hands]* What could be sweeter than the tales told about my reign! What have you got; I am all ears!

Shahrnâz: Then, come Arnavâz; I have never told a tale without you!

Arnavâz:	Shahrnâz — my sister — tell it without me, just this time! I am tired of acting out your tales!
Zahhâk:	Don't play hard to get; there's no way out!
Shahrnâz:	Come — he likes your sleeve swaying and skirt whirling; the flow of your fingers on the harp and your songs! Perhaps your arts will help me out.
Arnavâz:	I have butterflies in my stomach — no — my heart is leaping!
Shahrnâz:	The snakes are sleeping; Arnavâz — and we're awake. Come — you are his wife!
Arnavâz:	You're too!
Shahrnâz:	I am his wife's sister!
Arnavâz:	I am also his wife's sister when you are his wife!
Zahhâk:	What's this talking in codes? Aren't you *both* my wives and my wife's sisters; and the daughters of Jamshid, the Sun King, whom I cut in half with a saw!
Shahrnâz:	People say that Jam was not in the tree you cut and that before your saw or any other saw could cut him, he had gone to the afterlife branch by branch to fulfil the Lord's order and judge the dead — maybe he will one day judge you.
Zahhâk:	Judge me — Jamshid, the King of the other world — judge me in the afterlife? Who has said this profanity?

Arnavâz:	Who has not heard it?
Zahhâk:	Such a day may never be, I hope — no! *[Worried]* Did you say to fulfil the Lord's order?
Shahrnâz:	This is not a tale made by me, Zahhâk; it is one made by the same people whose brains are the food of your snakes!
Arnavâz:	Two a day!
Zahhâk:	Hum, this last one is good! Talk about my reign! Say something nicer, and I will have it carved on mountain rocks!
Arnavâz:	*[Shaping her two hands as two snakes, Zahhâk-like]* When speaking of conquests, who else can you talk about but Zahhâk the Mighty Owner of Ten Thousand horses?
Zahhâk:	*[Thumping his foot]* I, Zahhâk, triumphed over rebels, and this was carved onto mountain rocks.
Shahrnâz:	And carved onto you?
Zahhâk:	Did I not reduce my enemies to their knees and triumph over the world?
Shahrnâz:	Over all except Ahriman! The thousand-faced one who grappled with Jam and failed to defeat him but landed you in dirt with only three moves.
Zahhâk:	What you are saying is unknown to my ears!
Shahrnâz:	You soiled and salted and broke and bloodied and ruined and dried the springs!

You cut trees, Zahhâk; trees, each leaf of which had a life of its own; and each branch yielded a fruit or flower of its own!

Arnavâz: You made him furious, my sister; his eyes are bloodshot.

Shahrnâz: In my divine dream I have seen this fury. I have seen that flowing springs have dreamed of a bull-riding hero who will rebuild their beds and ducts, bludgeon your head with his mace, Zahhâk, and chain your demons.

Zahhâk: *[Unbelieving]* Such insolent nonsense — I have never heard or seen before!

Shahrnâz: *[Bends her head]* It is best if you take women's dreams as the opposite of what will be.

Zahhâk: Ha — So be it! *[Mocking]* The dream of a justice-worshiping new hero! *[Scared]* Ha — This was the dream that made me jump!

Arnavâz: Does fear still sound sweet to your ears?

Zahhâk: Envy will kill me if you give this kingship, that I have, to another!

Shahrnâz: Let's begin then Arnavâz; with this. With the two daughters of Jam, who wept in secret as clouds — trembling — for their lives when they heard of the saw and the slicing of their father in half!

Arnavâz: burr, burr, burr, burr, burr — burr, burr!

Zahhâk: *[Pleased]* I hear it now — ha — sawing the

huge tree!

Shahrnâz: And then when they heard of the snakes that had grown on your shoulders and the terror of Iran-land!

Arnavâz: Tsss — Tsss — Tsss — Tsss — !

Zahhâk: *[Pleased]* The hiss-hiss of my snakes! Ha-ha! Well done, you do it so well! For a moment, I thought they were awake! Well, what then?

Shahrnâz: What, what then?

Arnavâz: *[Falling on her knees]* All who had straightened their backs fell to their knees!

Zahhâk: What? Yea — all, everywhere the flags of the three headed dragon wave in the wind; and written testimonials have been put up on every corner, so people testify to my justness.

Shahrnâz: *[Circling around Arnavâz]* You, Jam's daughter! How much longer are you going to water the narcissus of your eyes? Bite your lips, pray to the Lord —

Arnavâz: In hiding; trembling for your life; weeping over the fate? *[Suddenly scared]* For sure, that dragon is looking for us!

Shahrnâz: Yes, Zahhâk — the son of my father's sister — if he is determined to take Jam's place, why should he leave his beautiful daughters alone? After all, we carry the divine right, the God-given royal excellence.

Arnavâz:	Sooner or later his spies will find this hiding place, and his agents will be behind the door?
Shahrnâz:	You Grand Priest — who read King Jamshid's orders, you or me?
Arnavâz:	I assume it was you!
Shahrnâz:	The idea was yours, wasn't it? Yes, it was! You said: "Oh, my Lord's daughter — what will become of this land? The land that the shining Jamshid expanded with justice, generosity and painful care!"
Zahhâk:	So you still reminisce about your father — and his goodness. *[Suspiciously]* Who else remembers him, and where? If he was Jam, I am Jam-ripper! I must send soldiers to mark their doors with painted hands to later feed their brains to our snakes.
Shahrnâz:	I said, "Oh sister, this snake-shouldered man is sitting on my father's throne, razing the land with his sword, and seeking the brains of the youths in spite.
Arnavâz:	I said, "Awful days, cursed spite! That's precisely why I am weeping!"
Zahhâk:	*[Unbelieving]* You said this, and you that?
Arnavâz:	I said, "Alas and alack those cares and pains that went into turning the lands of the ruined and none into the prosperous Iran.
Shahrnâz:	I said, "Alack and alas!"

Arnavâz:	*[Beating herself in dismay]* How much longer shall we shed tears of blood for this loss!
Shahrnâz:	I said, "Ask for the Royal Advisor, the Grand Priest, I may have a solution!" You said —
Arnavâz:	What — a solution?
Shahrnâz:	I said, "Call him Arnavâz, call him my sister!"
Zahhâk:	Hay — they're trying my patience. Patience, Zahhâk, you must listen.
Arnavâz:	*[With a different costume or a half mask]* I'm the advisor; my ladies — Your Highnesses — Leaders! What is your order, you, dear daughters of Jam? It pains me to see you trembling for your life.
Shahrnâz:	You great man — you, the head of all priests and the greatest of all priests! You were my father's advisor, and for us just like a father! Come and do something!
Arnavâz:	May I ask Shahrnâz of Jam to add this wisdom to her greatness that the best of deeds now is this very hiding which leads the three headed dragon to despair by confounding him! He sought you, the most shining beauties, with magic, but failing to find you he painted the days black as the colour of your eyes! He found and violently subdued your servants but assumed you had gone to Indian lands. He roared and fumed with rage, as he knew that the world watching sun has never seen a body purer

then your two pure bodies!

Shahrnâz: I am happy he was wailing, but doubtless his wailing is much less than the wailings of others.

Arnavâz: *[Bowing]* Then Your Highness! — My Lady — has also heard!

Shahrnâz: From every corner of the land wailings have reached the sky. Two a day! Two fifteen-year-olds — youths of pure souls!

Zahhâk: *[To his snakes]* You see, this infamy is because of you!

Arnavâz: An alien physician suddenly appeared this morning and said, "My King, I have the cure for your pain." And prescribed this remedy. When he left, we chased but failed to find him. And the dragon roared and did not accept any other physicians or any of the cures we recommended, as if despite all his magic, he had been bewitched by his magic.

Shahrnâz: Did you say we should make him suffer by hiding? No — that way we make our own hearts bleed every day as they drain the hearts and lives of mothers by beheading two youths. Come my other father — my advisor — do what I will tell you to do. We, Jams's daughters — Shahrnâz and Arnavâz — who were the sunshine of Jam's fortune and are now Zahhâk's ultimate dream; we wish to become the wives of the murderous Zahhâk.

Arnavâz: *[Shocked, he steps back in fear]* That tyrant?

Shahrnâz:	Yea, the very one with whose arrival peace departed the universe!
Zahhâk:	*[Agitated]* You called me "murderous", and you "tyrant"?
Arnavâz:	*[Screaming as herself]* No, Shahrnâz — my sister — don't ask or even say it.
Shahrnâz:	I will, my sister — and you also, be with me in this!
Arnavâz:	*[As the Priest]* How? Jam's curse will fall on me for such a scandal. Is it not a disgrace? Jam's daughters in Zahhâk's bed, sleeping with him?
Shahrnâz:	Upon my life, it is a disgrace — yes — but the greater disgrace is to hide and watch as every day they cut out the brains of two youths and feed them to his snakes to calm his anguish, the anguish of the hatreds in his head.
Zahhâk:	*[Forward and vengeful]* That haggard Grand priest-advisor, didn't he rage at you? Was he with you in this? Hah! I shall remember what you said!
Arnavâz:	*[Playing a terrified priest]* The All-knowing Just Lord knows that he has no access to you in this hiding place —
Zahhâk:	*[Twisting with rage]* Ungrateful Advisor! You reckless, stupid wretch! — playing two-face tricks on me!
Arnavâz:	*[She is baffled but continues as the Priest]* — But if

	you remain in hiding, it will be like keeping the sun in a pouch — laughter will vanish, and the black cold and the devastating Vayu wind will conquer the world.
Shahrnâz:	Did you say ruins, Grand priest? My Advisor, ruining is Zahhâk's job, not ours. How much longer shall we hide when people's flesh and blood are under his fangs?
Arnavâz:	[As herself] You can say that again! The Zahhâk that I know will not stop his tyranny until we show ourselves.
Zahhâk:	Ha, Zahhâk; what tricks did they play to get into your inner room; and you thought your magic that brought them back; and said, "What a conquest to finally bring these silver-bodied beauties to your inner room!"
Shahrnâz:	Were we not your ultimate wish? Didn't you say, "I would shade their sunshine bodies with my dragon body so the earth would remain in dark, and the whole world would shake of the terror of my power."
Zahhâk:	My snakes, keep calm. Do not roar or rumble! There are many things that I still don't know. This story is indeed other than the other thousand nights!
Arnavâz:	[As the Priest] Your Highnesses — My ladies — you know that he cannot have the ring of kingship except by marrying you? [Being herself — obstinate and bitter] Oh! My close kin,

Zahhâk, the son of my father's sister, say, did
you not send night seekers and day guards
to seek us, for your own bed? And did you
not say that our bodies are the best for your
passion and for easing the spite you have
against Jam.

Shahrnâz: Did they not tell you the kingship has been
trusted to Jam's daughters and no man
could become king, unless by marrying the
Lord's daughters?

Zahhâk: *[Angrily to himself]* More venom than this?
Hah — words mixed with venom! My snakes,
keep calm, I shall know more.

Arnavâz: *[As the Priest — restless]* No — I won't commit
such an evil deed! My lady, Shahrnâz of Jam,
will you not despair of the words that will ring
around this tight world about this disgrace,
such words that — frozen be my tongue —
would trample your name with infamy?

Shahrnâz: That is also a pain that must be borne.

Arnavâz: *[Continuing]* Is it not inflicting disgrace on
yourself if you voluntarily step in the path of
harm? Is it not better to be taken by force
than willingly?

Shahrnâz: No, my Grand Priest, my advisor; my second
father, no!

Arnavâz: *[As herself]* Do you not heed my sister that if
we are taken by force, we will be seen as
two of the oppressed, and if we go willingly

	as partners of oppression?
Shahrnâz:	It is better if they see me as a partner of oppression if it helps me diminish it. May there never be a day I am seen as one of the oppressed if it increases oppression!
Zahhâk:	*[Laughing]* Women are unwise even if they are Jam's daughters.
Shahrnâz:	Listen, my sister — if that beast knows of our spite and learns that we are seeking a way to flee, when we are caught by force, we will be at his mercy and the slaves of his suspicion. He will assign spies and interrogators for us, and we will be unable to do anything. So let him assume we are enthralled by him. Yes, my father — our advisor — tell him that our feminine desire craves his snakes and his unruly power before which chastity drops its shield. Tell him you heard us praise him because all men hide the snakes of their spiteful natures, but he, being the only one who revealed his snakes, is the only honest man. Tell him we are hiding because we are afraid of his saw, the very saw with which he killed our father; otherwise, every night we pass our time thinking about and craving him.
Zahhâk:	Hah! Yea; you had no way, but to come to my hands on your own feet! *[Roaring]* This is a tale which my people have not yet carved onto mountains!
Arnavâz:	*[As the Priest]* Oh God take my life; what is

this I am hearing from Jam's daughters. Has his magic affected you? Is this sacrifice or enthrallment! My head be the dust of your soles, do you really intend to give your hands to that bizarre, demonic creature? Hah — what enthralment, curse or magic can make two heavenly beauties go to the mouth of a dragon that they are sacred of?

Shahrnâz: *[Bitterly]* Humm! — for sure we will be judged as you just said, Grand Priest-advisor; but we have no way to avoid this venom. Reparation, my sister, we shall pay reparation! So let me finish this! My Grand Priest-advisor, know that if that dragon is craving to have us, I am also a woman and see a passion for him in all parts of my body; for that covetous vindictive body; for that coarse dark skin, and those insatiable snakes! Now, how does it feel to go to bed with snakes? How? Do they sting or break the bones or curl around you and push through? Well, yes, we shall be two-faced, my sister! We will be forced to go, so why should we not make him think we go willingly? My second father, tell him we are enthralled by the three headed dragon and will touch the moon of honour by this marriage!

Arnavâz: *[As the Priest]* Shame on me — Is there any deed worse than this in the world?

Shahrnâz: Yes, this is the worst thing I have ever done, yet it is better than watching and doing nothing! How much longer shall we go on growing our harvests with the blood of the slayed and then see them burned for nothing? It has been prophesized that his kingship will be time-bound, and that Irânshahr will have no way to escape his magic. Thus, we shall end this chaotic era of between-kings by crowning him. Once he is the King, the count of his time-bound era will begin!

Zahhâk: *[Unbelieving, slowly rising]* The count of my time-bound era?

Arnavâz: *[As the Priest, she puts her hand on her heart]* Oh, the Judge of the other world — Jam — forgive me for wrongly judging your daughters!

Shahrnâz: I heard it from you, priests, that you have seen in the stars he will have a thousand days of kingship; so if I can rescue a thousand youths from his carnage, why should I consider my name or life more valuable than that?

Zahhâk: *(Confused]* A thousand days? Hah — they told me a thousand years!

Arnavâz: *[As herself]* Oh Zahhâk! Every day of your rule was like a year to us. Do not deceive yourself with the words of astrologers!

Zahhâk: *[Frightened]* Is every year of the star of luck a day or a night for us? And was today really the one thousandth day?

Arnavâz: *[As the Priest, she puts the crown on Zahhâk's head]* Then, let him begin his one thousand days with this three-chinned, six-eyed crown that goes on his head.

Zahhâk: Did the dead-end day come in a blinking of an eye? The very last day! The one thousand and first day? Why is the strength of my body gone, and the vigour of my wisdom wilted?

Arnavâz: *[As the Priest, bowing]* I will marry you to that sorcerer, my ladies!

Shahrnâz: Well, no; I will mesmerize his magic. Yea, I have concocted a fine plan. You, Grand Priest-advisor! He will only have us in his dreams! Be our father and give our hands to him in marriage; and let him assume we are enthralled by his magic!

Arnavâz: *[Anxious]* My sister, how is it possible to transform a demonic man who does not discern good from evil with a plan? How is it possible to make a covetous man, whose avarice has plagued the world, turn from evil to good?

Shahrnâz: With toil and resolution, my sister. And if compassion and wisdom did not transform his conduct and beliefs, what else can we do but seek a just man — a human-loving person — and grant him the title and the throne! Yet time is needed to reveal the unjustness of this and the justness of the other to the world. From good to evil is a purgatory, my sister — in which we are now!

Arnavâz: *[As the Priest, bowing]* Your Highness — My

lady, consider it done!

Zahhâk: I remember. That pimp, your grand priest-advisor, came and said, "I found them! Or maybe they themselves wished to be found but with some hardship to make sure you really remember and want them." Yea, he then received some reward and said, "I found the treasure that is befitting of your snakes." *[Confused]* You became my wives to shake the pillars of my power?

Shahrnâz: We became your wives to diminish the burden of your tyranny on the world and tell you that there is also justice and bounty in the world.

Zahhâk: Justice and bounty? I am Zahhâk!

Shahrnâz: We said the same thing! If you were Jamshid, the world would be different!

Zahhâk: For me justice is to remain seated on the throne and be tended by the world as tributes arrive from everywhere to glorify my grandeur. It is to have my snakes guarding me and pouring venom into the lives of my enemies, as I feed them with the brain of youths! Hah — this grand priest-advisor of yours will not live to see the light of tomorrow — the henpecked wretch. *[Frightened]* Is there really a tomorrow for me — or — is this the one thousand and first one? *[Brushing away his fear]* No! What nonsense?

Shahrnâz: *[To Arnavâz/Priest]* Another thing, call for

	Jamshid's chefs. They were a married couple, excellent chefs and faithful — and reliable with our secrets!
Arnavâz:	*[As the Priest. Scared]* What is this? Toying with your life? This is naught but throwing your life away!
Shahrnâz:	Should there not be people to set feast tables at our command splendidly as customary and prepare colourful food of all types? If it were not for Jamshid's name, who presides over the world of darkness, I would light the stove with my own hands and every night would make his eyelids heavy by putting some medicine into his food.
Arnavâz:	*[As the Priest]* Then you would die before him as his food taster.
Shahrnâz:	Do not worry yourself over us, my father advisor! Just say these spoiled girls do not touch anything that has not been cooked by these chefs! Say if you want to replace the sun-like Jamshid, take all together: his throne and crown, his bed, his daughters, his advisor, and his chefs.
Zahhâk:	*[Confused]* Where was my magic to reveal these secrets!
Arnavâz:	*[As the Priest]* I am worried about your lives. Shahrnâz, Arnavâz, the Lord's daughters, do you not know that Ahriman is in him and his protector, and warns him when needed?

Then, listen to know that the arch-evil-doer first appeared to Zahhâk, a madly ambitious man, as a wizard and taught him all forms of dark magic and having enthralled him with the allure of power asked him to kill his father as his payment. And Zahhâk killed and replaced his father! Another day he appeared to him as a chef and presented him with so many tasty foods that Zahhâk offered to give him a reward. And he asked to kiss his shoulders, and he did. And from the two places two snakes which terrified and tortured Zahhâk making him growl and roar in pain and take sword and massacre many. And Jam fled from him until he reached that tree! Then Ahriman appeared again as a physician and told him that the medicine for calming the snakes — and saving him from them — was the brains of two youths — taken out, marinated and cooked as food for them. And Zahhâk was pleased with this cure and commanded his people to have it done. And thus, he became a slave of Ahriman. You may not know, but poison has no effect on him, and because of his snakes, it is not possible to jump on him with a dagger? Because when he is asleep, they are awake and guard him, and when his snakes sleep, he is awake, all covered in blades and with magic?

Zahhâk: *[Brandishing his sword]* Hah! — yea; what a beautiful word is fear! And you are more beautiful when you are terrified. Am I not right?

Shahrnâz: Yes, my father — advisor, I have no hope, no more than nothing. My kin, Zahhâk, the son of Jamshid's sister from a foreign man, killed his own father, Mardâs, slept with his own mother, and killed his mother's brother — our father — with a saw and crushed Irânshahr under his tyranny. So why shall we who are also from Irânshahr choose comfort and separate ourselves from others? Act like a father for us and do this. I shall put the evil inside him to sleep every night — like a baby — with a lullaby and will ask the chefs to set the two youths free.

Zahhâk: What unheard things! What unknown stories!

Arnavâz: Oh, no, no, which chef would risk becoming firewood for such a stove!

Shahrnâz: No one, of course, if they are not heartbroken with the atrocities around them! And for now, until Irânshahr will make its own cure by the hands of the manly men it breeds, what other cure do we have?

Arnavâz: [As the Priest, bowing] The chefs are here.

Zahhâk: [Anxiously] No — this is not the tale of other nights. This is a nightmare I am having while awake.

Shahrnâz: I can leave it halfway if the nightmare is too agonizing.

Zahhâk:	No — tell me more, more! How can I ever sleep again or not sleep, when everything has been a chimera!
Shahrnâz:	Are you a chef?
Arnavâz:	*[As the chef]* Your servant!
Shahrnâz:	Who am I, then, if you are my servant?
Arnavâz:	You are King Zahhâk's wife!
Shahrnâz:	Thus, you know well why I am so worried about my dear husband's food. Are you the one who cooks his snakes' food?
Arnavâz:	This hardest of jobs — yes — it is my job, my lady! *[Crying]* The other chefs all hate and avoid it, so this *[Biting his hand]* evil, ominous work has been left to me, this ill-fated man!
Shahrnâz:	So the chef of this food suffers from fashioning it. Are you really unhappy? Are the tears in your eyes not fake, kind man?
Arnavâz:	*[Hesitant]* And your tears?
Shahrnâz:	Well, if you are the one who once liked us, perhaps may name has not elapsed your mind!
Arnavâz:	Please let it be, my lady. I am dumb. Please, do not ask and do not hear me — my lady. *[Kneeling and kissing her skirt]* All our life we have lived on the bounty of your table.
Shahrnâz:	And now you are afraid of uttering my name! Was I not somebody before you know me as the wife of that three-headed, three-jawed,

six-eyed dragon?

Arnavâz: You are the daughter of Jam — who cleansed
            Iran of demonic *divan*!

Shahrnâz: So now that a demon is over us, think of me
            as what I was and answer; are you the one
            preparing the food of his snakes?

Arnavâz: Not of my own accord, but with tearful eyes.

Shahrnâz: Did you try to see if the snakes calm down
            with sheep's or ewe's brains?

Zahhâk: What, my chef — following your orders?

Arnavâz: *[Terrified]* My lady — You seem unaware and
            unafraid of his ears which are also six in
            number.

Shahrnâz: Do not fear. He is now preoccupied with my
            sister. Yea — he has released his snakes on
            her. Listen — you, esteemed man — they are
            making together — like two harmoniously
            tuned instruments — one high- and one
            low-pitched the most pleasant melody of
            the world!

Arnavâz: Forgive my impertinence, your highness,
            but please abstain from envy!

Shahrnâz: And you more than I! I assumed men would
            be envious if an ugly demon was embracing
            the most beautiful fairy of the world and
            consummating his lust.

Arnavâz: *[Envious]* That aside, my lady — *[crying]* There are plenty of men who sigh from their hearts!

Zahhâk: Ha Ha — I have branded the hearts of your men with my burning rod, haven't I? My snakes rejoice in slithering on your curves, and the men who crave you are displeased.

Arnavâz: *[Shouting angrily at the sky]* How can I be pleased when the dragon of dark clouds is covering the moon?

Shahrnâz: Say then — have you tried to use sheep brains instead of human brains for the snakes?

Arnavâz: They had tried it before us, my lady — with sheep brains, the snakes sting and spit venom, and bite wildly, making the insane man growl and draw his bloodthirsty massacre blade!

Shahrnâz: Hum! You made me lose hope! But you did not say if you tried just one brain?

Arnavâz: Just one head and one brain!?

Shahrnâz: *[Anxious]* Or mixing it with the brain of a sheep or ewe or a donkey! For God's sake, do not add distrust and doubt to our problems and tell me with no fear! You have a wife who is your teacher in these skills; ask her to find a way; and she, being a mother, will find a good way to do it. Oh — see how I am haggling for the lives of those whose lives have become so cheap since this dragon sat on the throne! Say — are you going to try this straightaway?

Arnavâz:	Oh, daughter of the Lord, attired in fire and water — the guards watch with wide, gory eyes; and the snakes, if they do not calm down with one brain, he will have my own brain cooked!
Shahrnâz:	I will risk my life if you have the heart. The guards also fear for their lives! First, say one of them escaped and when they run to catch him, let the other go, and make the food. If the food is enough for the snakes and they calm down, the guards will no longer fear and will cooperate; and some gold coins may also help, which I will give you from my hair pendants.
Zahhâk:	*[Looking from behind a blanket, which he is holding like a wall]* What tricks in your pockets and what hoaxes in your sleeves you have!
Arnavâz:	This secret will not remain hidden — no! He sometimes checks on things unexpectedly, my lady. What shall we do then?
Shahrnâz:	We will deal with that. We use our female intuition to lull his magic to sleep; we will teach him humanity. I will use my brain in place of the second youth. Each night I will make something up to distract him.
Zahhâk:	Something?
Arnavâz:	Playing the harp or flute? Sleeve swaying and skirt whirling!
Shahrnâz:	Matched and tuned with a poem, a song!

Zahhâk:	*[With resentment]* Hah! Advice and guidance?
Arnavâz:	*[As the chef]* On what is worthy and what unworthy?
Zahhâk:	Hum! *[Suspicious]* A charm?
Arnavâz:	A tale?
Zahhâk:	Of a hero whose mother was a cow — and of the one-night king!
Arnavâz:	Yes — if you take one for a thousand!
Shahrnâz:	This may work if the tale is alluring! I, the one, who is his wife's sister and his wife, and my sister, who is his wife and his wife's sister; oh yes — we will find a way to entertain him, to decrease his agony and anxiety and meanwhile you save the life of one of the two! Give wine to the guards, water to the victim, and bread to the fugitive!
Arnavâz:	What a strange way to toy with death! How shall I choose one of the two?
Shahrnâz:	*[Turning her head in pain. To herself]* Be harsh, daughter of the Lord — swallow your grief and do not cry — *[She manages to control her emotions]* Let them choose between themselves; I know it is hard for a caring man like you to choose one over the other.
Zahhâk:	*[Mocking — as the chef]* I wish I never see your rosy face sad!
Shahrnâz:	Any young man shouts when the blade is on

his throat — until the artery is cut! That blood-sucking tyrant may prick his ears for the second one; and may become suspicious if he does not hear it. So — yes — each night give a shout similar to the groan of the dying victim, so we know it is done!

[The loud crying of Arnavâz]

Zahhâk: *[Mocking — as the chef]* I wish I never see the tears of my lady!

Shahrnâz: Each night will be a test of my nerves when the dying one shrieks the cry of death to the sky!

Zahhâk: *[Mocking — as the chef]* I wish my lady's fast-beating heart and the blood running to her eyes do not expose her!

Arnavâz: *[Confused]* What tale will it be when told under the blade!

Shahrnâz: And can I actually do it? You do not know how hard it is to go to bed with the enemy! And how hard to hear the death cries of your people, while improvising a reviving tale and asking oneself why am I leaning on soft cushions as one of my people is under the blade of the one I am amusing!?

Arnavâz: *[As the chef]* I know — yes — hard; as hard as killing a brother; and cooking his brain for the enemy's snakes!

Zahhâk: *[Catching them red-handed]* You traitors — aha!

	You counted your sins, Shahrnâz; and you Arnavâz!
Shahrnâz:	Betraying a traitor is loyalty to the good, Zahhâk — did you not know that?
Zahhâk:	You and you became my wives and my wives' sisters to overthrow me!? You and you and that grand priest-advisor and that ungrateful chef conspired against me, your husband!?
Shahrnâz:	You are right, Zahhâk! This was in response to your pact with the devil to destroy Iran, to kill Jam with a saw, and to slay the youths and to take their brains out! You, blood-thirsty tyrant, should blame yourself. You became the nest for the demon of avarice and your ambition borrowed its wings from the devil!
Zahhâk:	Well, I know what to do! The grand priest-advisor's and the chef's would be the two brains that feed my snakes tomorrow.
Arnavâz:	*[Mocking him]* You always looked for young brains!
Zahhâk:	Yes, the brains of their young ones! You, chef, consider yourself boiled in the pot and your bones thrown to dogs! And you, grand priest-advisor, shall I throw you down a well, or have you hanged or executed by an archery squad? Ha! You unmanly man — obeying women. And you, two. No, I will not break my kingship by killing you. You are Jam's daughters and possess the God-given

Royal Brilliance! For you traitors — you ungrateful wretches — I have another plan and will make you suffer night and day!

Shahrnâz: Ungrateful is the one who killed his father and slept with his mother; killed his mother's brother with a saw and took his daughters to his bed; and cut the brains of Irânshahr's youth out of their heads for his snakes. I cared for my father, my land, and the youths of Irânshahr. I accepted infamy by marrying the enemy to uphold my gratitude to all these and protect them.

Arnavâz: *[Performing and also complaining]* Alas! Zahhâk, you do not know what it is to go to bed with two snakes and a man.

Zahhâk: And you do not know how it feels to go to bed with two women; women who are the daughters of your enemy, and so close to you! The daughters of your mother's brother; women whom you craved since childhood! Yes, you do not know what it feels like to go to bed with two silver-bodied beauties and to remain unsure which to take to get the most out of it.

Shahrnâz: You did not get the most out of it, Zahhâk, your snakes did.

Zahhâk: What?

Shahrnâz: When you slept, your snakes kept eyeing me or ogling my sister's pure body! Sometimes

	so avidly that we thought they might sting you to get rid of you, Zahhâk.
Zahhâk:	*[Confused]* What? Is it true?
Arnavâz:	You see, even your snakes were not free, Zahhâk!
Zahhâk:	No, I refuse to believe it! Oh Zahhâk, did you ever ask yourself how for a thousand nights you went into bed with two beautiful-bodied women and none of them showed you a baby?
Arnavâz:	Do you really think you slept with us for a thousand nights?
Zahhâk:	You pretended you had given birth to two boys!
Shahrnâz:	Oh Zahhâk, we made myriads of tales to entertain you?
Zahhâk:	Tales?
Shahrnâz:	Which of them did you not like? Every night as soon as your pains were relieved you fell asleep, Zahhâk!
Arnavâz:	Every night when you fell asleep, your snakes embraced us.
Shahrnâz:	Do you think it was easy to sleep in the embrace of your snakes for a thousand nights?
Arnavâz:	These snakes which are awake when you are asleep and asleep when you are awake!
Zahhâk:	*[Ordering the snakes]* Now is the time; the time of retribution! Turn them into ash! Ashes under my feet, though I already see

myself in despair in the ashes of the fire that burns these two beauties. *[Confused]* My snakes, what is wrong with you? *[Terrified]* Why do they not obey me?

Shahrnâz: Did you really think they obeyed you rather than the other way round?

Zahhâk: Hah — *[Taking out his sword]* If my snakes do not obey me, my sword will!

Shahrnâz: Don't! — because if you bring that down, your remorse will be useless; and what happened to the Indian gamekeeper will happen to you.

Zahhâk: *[His hand and sword remain above his head]* What — *[Going backward and sitting on the throne]* What is this tale?

Shahrnâz: In a distant place in India, in a beautiful valley, where the forest, the meadow and the river joined each other, there was a narrow-minded, quick-tempered man, whose name was Koupal of Shangal.

[At the same time, Arnavâz begins her performance by bringing her two hands together and then stepping in and twirling while twisting her imaginary moustache]

— He bred and trained falcons for the noblemen and rajahs and was the greatest of masters in his trade. And he had a lovely wife, virtuous and one of a kind in gentility and beauty, so that even mirrors were embarrassed by so much charm!

[At the same time, Arnavâz plays the mirror and the woman and then the distrust of the falconer]

— And the woman told the man to find a cure for his quick temper! Yet the man was blind to the worth of her words, and always thought, "when I am busy with my falcons — caring for their chicks in the nests — or landing them from the sky and taming them, what does this beauty do, a woman with these exquisite features, with whom does she play the backgammon of love? He suffered more with these thoughts as he knew that even gods desired her. Thus, he questioned the woman several times, and each time the woman said, "When you are not here, I care for the chicks, making them happy with seeds and water and giving them of my own food." Yet the man was not satisfied with this answer!

[While telling the tale, Shahrnâz joins Arnavâz, each depicting one or the other of the characters]

— One day in his absence a poor woman passed their door, a foul-smelling woman of the untouchable cast, with tattered clothes. The woman was kind to her and gave her a bit of food and some clothes, not knowing that the man had the counts of everything and had a list with him. When the tricky man returned and looked for the things, a few things were missing from the house, and he assumed that the woman had an affair with an adept philanderer! He scorned, cursed and showered the woman with harsh questions. The woman told the tale of the untouchable old woman, but the man being mistrustful by nature did not believe her and went for his whip and sword to make her talk. The untouchable old woman appeared and warned him to still his sword, saying "harming this woman is like bringing down your house on your head! The man stopped his ears, moved his sword, and slayed the woman! The falcon chicks, instantly, began to cry and shriek. They broke from their cage and lunged at him, picking out his eyes and tearing his flesh and skin apart! Then, the old woman in tatters, who was in fact the fairy of the lovely woman and had come to test her, healed her in a moment. Yet it was too late for the falconer to know that the birds, unhappy with him, had fallen in love with his beloved wife due to her gentility and compassion!

Zahhâk: *[Dropping his sword. Suspicious]* Ha! My snakes! Mine as parts of my body!

Arnavâz: Beware of them, Zahhâk, for your life!

Zahhâk: *[Growling at the snakes]* I wish you had tongues to tell me what happened between you when I was asleep.

[Shahrnâz and Arnavâz hide their smiles with the back of their hands]

Zahhâk: *[Takes his spear]* You tried for a thousand nights to fool my snakes! You fairy-like beauties with whose delicate steps my snakes forgot their venom!

Arnavâz: They were intoxicated with our scent.

Zahhâk: *[Suspicious]* And you did not stab me with the dagger I have at my side!

Shahrnâz: How? Your slithering snakes coiled and curled round us caressing and loving in such ways that their venom turned into honey in our palates.

Zahhâk: *[Furious]* Do not set me against my snakes!

Shahrnâz: Your enemies are your snakes, Zahhâk.

Zahhâk: *[Roaring]* Do not inject envy into my soul! *[Roaring and controlling himself]* Hah! You two beauties, in the tales you made you pretended you gave birth to two children for me!

Arnavâz: He wants children from us, Shahrnâz — say something!

Shahrnâz: Oh! — you do not know how hard it is to give birth to a child that you hate!

Zahhâk: You hate? I want my children — two boys.

Shahrnâz: Looking for your children, Zahhâk? Your little youths!? Can you take it? You say it, Arnavâz!

Arnavâz:	No — you say it; you are the one with so many tales.
Shahrnâz:	This very last night — tonight — we calmed down your snakes with the brains of your two children!
Zahhâk:	*[Shocked]* You are not telling the truth!
Shahrnâz:	We gave birth to two snakes, Zahhâk; and one Zahhâk was enough for this world!
Zahhâk:	You snake-stung women are stinging me! Please, let it not be right, do not say you crushed their heads!
Shahrnâz:	They were the children of your snakes — not you!
Zahhâk:	Which is me and which my snakes? Which is the truth and which the tale? Oh Zahhâk, you were naive, tricked by these women — and if devil is my friend, he was also tricked by them!
Shahrnâz:	We gave birth to a thousand and one children!
Arnavâz:	A thousand and one youths escaped, one every night when we lulled you to sleep and woke your snakes up. And now you are in the coil of their siege. They have come to revenge the death of their murdered relatives!
Zahhâk:	*[Shocked with despair]* You are lying!
Arnavâz:	Look form these windows, Zahhâk. Outside

you will see a thousand and one fires. A thousand and one manly men, coming, brandishing swords! Is it not the time your snakes sting themselves, or sting you before themselves?

Zahhâk: *[Terrified]*. They are hammering the ground with their spears. I am entrapped! *[Shouting]* There is no way out! *[Crying]* Am I not your relative?

Shahrnâz: You did not say this when wielding your saw to cut our father into half!

Zahhâk: *[Snatching his sword]* I will not say it when slaying you! You who gave birth to a thousand and one children to capture me! *[His hands fall back]* Oh — why does my magic have no effect on you? Did you really allure and trick my snakes? Yes, I must beware of my snakes because though they were once with me, they are no longer so!

Shahrnâz: You, snake-worshipper! You are the nurse of your snakes. I gave you the cure. I told you to starve and weaken your snakes, to get rid of them so people could befriend you, but you did not. What else could I do but give the ring of kingship to a just king who is not the nest of snakes and whose greatest suffering is the suffering of people!

Zahhâk: They are closer! Where are the castle guards and soldiers!

Shahrnâz:	Throw the ropes, take off the bolts and open the gates, Arnavâz. The dream of the flowing, freshwater springs is being fulfilled.
Zahhâk:	*[Terrified]* Hah!
Shahrnâz:	In my divine dream I nurtured a hero — just —
Arnavâz:	A brave man, riding on the wind with hands of flowing waters!
Shahrnâz:	Walking on the earth and passing through the fire!
Arnavâz:	A hero whose mother was a cow!
Shahrnâz:	Who is coming to revive the springs and the trees!
Arnavâz:	*[Putting chains on Zahhâk's neck]* It is time you put your head in the pillory, Zahhâk, as your palace guards and bodyguards have all thrown their swords down and escaped!
Zahhâk:	*[On his knees]* Your name will be erased! You are stupid! Heroes will come and chain me; and you will get naught but censure for being my wives! In the tales they tell about the battle, there will be no words about you; yes — in the victory that will come, no one will even remember you!
Shahrnâz:	I did not do this for name, Zahhâk; neither did my sister Arnavâz. We are Jam's daughters; we adorn the world with justice and are cut into death with saws of injustice.

The
One Thousand and First Night
2

Characters:

Khurzâd-e Nikrokh [Prosecutor]

Mâhak [Head of the Police]

Sheriff / The Iranian [Pour-e Farrokhân] / *Grand Warden*

The Stage:

A sturdy double door with doorknobs and doorknockers in its solid frame! Both sides are fully open, and a purple curtain with blue margins is draped behind it. In front of the door, on a tree stump in the middle of a square platform, is sitting the King of Merchants, The Sheriff of Baghdad, holding up a leather covered book. Further to the front, sitting on the ground are two women in long loose-fitting, cloak-like, dark blue and light turquoise covers; both are anxious and agitated.

Sheriff: Then this is the original!

Khurzâd: Yes — your highness, it is the original!

Sheriff: This and no other.

Khurzâd: I confirm, my wise master. May your life and
              glory be eternal! Yes — it is the very one he
              translated.

Mâhak: [Showing the book] Hezâr Afsân!

Sheriff: What does that mean?

Khurzâd: A Thousand Tales![1] My honourable master,
              where is he himself?

Sheriff: Himself?

              [Khurzâd looks at Mâhak. Mâhak quickly brings
              out a piece of paper from her sleeve]

---

1. Alef al-Qesas

Mâhak: *[Reading from the paper]* This message is from me, Pour-e Farrokhân —

Sheriff: *[Reminding them]* Who was called the Son of Auspicious in translation![1]

Mâhak: *[Confused, she reads]* the Son of Mazdak-e Dabir —

Sheriff: Whose name was translated as the Son of Jerjis, the Scribe![2]

Mâhak: *[More confused and then hastily]* To my beloved wife, Khurzâd —

Sheriff: Read as the Daughter of the Sun.[3]

Mâhak: *[Confused, to Khurzâd]* I wonder why he has called you with your maiden name!

Khurzâd: *[To the Sheriff]* Her brother called me Nikrokh!

Sheriff: Say Good-Looking![4]

Mâhak: Oh — *[She goes back to the letter]* And my sister, Mâhak —

Sheriff: Correct it to Crescent.[5]

Khurzâd: *[Hastily]* Read the rest.

Mâhak: I am writing to ask for that unique old book.

---

1. Ibn-e Meimoon
2. Ibn-e Jerjis al-Kâteb
3. Bento-Shshams
4. Vajiheh
5. Helal al-Qamar.

Khurzâd:	*[She hastily shows the book]* Hezâr Afsân!
Sheriff:	Say the meaning!
Mâhak:	The same she said.
Khurzâd:	*A Thousand Tales!*
Sheriff:	The auditor counted. The tales were not a thousand!
Mâhak:	This is an Iranian custom; they say a thousand when they mean many; not that there are actually a thousand.
Khurzâd:	His Highness is aware of this!
Sheriff:	With no exaggeration, of course! Is it possible that there are any other copies of this?
Khurzâd:	No, not really, we have not seen any.
Mâhak:	*[To Khurzâd]* I have seen — *[To the Sheriff]* with my own eyes. Oh — what a jewel! So beautifully written and well designed! In Ray, *[to the Sheriff]* which I think you have been to. I saw it, yes; it was in the fire during the book burning! Thanks to my brother, Pour-e Farrokh —
Sheriff:	*[Relieved]* Son of Auspicious!
Mâhak:	Oh, no — *[with difficulty]* Yes, who had already copied it himself!
Khurzâd:	Our justice-seeking master knows; the fire was the work of the governor about whose tyranny we came here to complain!

Sheriff:	God Forbid! — You did not say anything about the storerooms of Magus books in Persian!
Mâhak:	*[Quietly to Khurzâd]* No, they were not religious books, so they did not salvage them!
Sheriff:	Alas and a thousand times alas! Bring forward that bucket of water. I am hot!
Khurzâd:	*[Fanning herself]* Baghdad and its summers! You should thank God if you don't suffer fevers and chills!

[Mâhak quickly rises to look for water and finally brings forward a half-full cube-shaped bucket which has four handles on its four sides]

Sheriff:	*[He fans himself with the book]* So, you are certain there are no other copies!
Khurzâd:	*[She points to the book]* Except that there are definitely no other copies!
Mâhak:	*[Wile bringing the bucket]* In Ray, people say, "Two books are enough for a wise person; *Apestâk*,[1] which is the book of the heavens, and *Hezâr Afsân* which is a book of the earth.
Sheriff:	As for me, the Sheriff of Baghdad, I really enjoyed reading it. The scribes are all overjoyed and interested; looking for the original to check the meanings and the accuracy of the translation.
Mâhak:	*[Quietly to Khurzâd]* But they do not know

---

[1] Avesta, the Zoroastrian scriptures.

	Pahlavi![1]
Sheriff:	Unfortunately, of course! — who does?
Khurzâd:	To be exact, this Mâhak here and my husband Pour-e Farrokhân —
Sheriff:	Say the meaning!
Khurzâd:	*[Confused]* Oh, what was it? He called you "Crescent" and my husband, "Son of Auspicious", Son of Jerjis the Scribe of Ray"![2]
Sheriff:	Yes, much better; and preferable.
Khurzâd:	In Iran people are forgetting Pahlavi and have mixed it with Arabic in their trading talks — I know, as I had to sell some of my handiwork to earn a living!
Sheriff:	The language of trade, of course, should be Arabic, the most erudite and eloquent one in all its aspects; in the past and present — all over the world!
Mâhak:	*[Upset and obstinate]* The people of Ray call it the language of force!
Sheriff:	God knows better! *[To Khurzâd]* You said that this is nothing but *A Thousand Tales*, but your husband, Son of Auspicious, son of Jerjis — *[To Mâhak]* That is your brother. — *[To Khurzâd]* had put it as *A Thousand and One Night* in his

---

1. The script in which Middle Persian was written. The term was also used for the language.
2. Ibn-e Meimoon Ibn-e Jerjis al-Kateb al-Razi.

translation. Just tell me a tale from the book, to make sure we are talking about the same book or different ones!

Khurzâd: Her renowned name is Shahrzâd; she has a sister called Dinâzâd. They are the vizier's daughters, I think. They look for a way to stop a distrustful king who marries a virgin every night and kills her in the morning. This Shahrzâd shrewdly volunteers to become his wife for a night, but with Dinâzâd's help entertains the king with the magic of words at his bedtime for one thousand nights to distract him from killing virgins. Thus, she saves one thousand and one young girls from the blades of swordsmen and executioners.

Sheriff: Brilliant! *[He throws the book into the bucket]* Which sovereign among the governors is this evil man who relies so much on his throne?

[Mâhak and Khurzâd almost rise in panic. Mâhak gives a muffled scream, looks at Khurzâd and the bucket and turns her face wailing. Khurzâd extends her hands, with a lump in her throat, goes forward on her knees as if to save the book and hits herself on the head —]

Khurzâd: *[Hiding her fury and bitterness]* No — no sarcasm against the Arabs! The Magi say it dates back to Zahhâk's era; and the upstart scholars say one of the Sassanid kings! *[To Mâhak]* Don't they? *[To the Sheriff]* In the end — the king comes to his senses. Is this a problem?

Sheriff:	*[Looking at the bucket]* It's a brilliant story, an excellent account! His Highness, the Caliph heard it from the grand vizier, and he, from the head of ambassadors, and he, from the grand warden, and he from me — the head of all merchants — who had heard about the merits of this account throughout the world, in every corner of the earth. All were interested and eager to hear and yearning to read! The head of Caliph's library assigned me this duty; and this humblest, the head of all merchants, the Sheriff of Baghdad, humbly shouldered the payment of these one thousand and one Moroccan dinars — red gold — so that the people's treasury is not burdened by the amount!
Khurzâd:	*[Gazing at the bucket]* Now, they can say that this book did not exist!
Mâhak:	*[Gazing at the bucket]* This unique book: *Hezâr Afsân*.
Sheriff:	Destiny's decree! Heaven's verdict! You yourself brought the bucket forward! And I want the best for you, out of heartfelt compassion and tenderness!
Khurzâd:	The best for us?
Sheriff:	If the original had been discovered, your husband, Son of Auspicious, Son of Jerjis, could have been accused of the unforgivable crime of mixing our religion with the views of paltry fire-worshipers, which is, indeed, a

57

great blasphemy!

Khurzâd: *[Terrified by imagining what she is saying]* And now that the original is no longer there, he can be accused of pre-meditated, intentional, heresy, which is not a lesser crime, and in both cases spilling the sinner's blood is permitted.

Mâhak: *[Terrified]* What will happen to my brother!

Khurzâd: *[Passionately]* Hah — no! He translated the book into Arabic at your behest! For three years we lived in sheer, dog-like paucity, content with dry bread so that he can make a new life with the wage of this work and becomes worthy of the hearing and acceptance of His Just Highness, the Caliph!

Mâhak: The appeals are still here — listen, please — *[Rummaging through documents]* This is a letter from Pour-e Farrokhân, the Son of Mazdak-e Behdâd, from Ray to the Chief Justice of the City of Faith, Baghdad — *[Cutting some words]* The unjust governor considers us serf slaves, calls us non-Arab aliens, forces us to speak Arabic, burns books, destroys our water ducts on purpose, digs into our taxes for gold and sends mediating madams to seduce our wives and daughters. We all have complaints about our belongings being taken by force and sold —

Khurzâd: *[Worrying that she is going too far]* The Sheriff of Baghdad has, of course, been to Iran in person and has heard about the numerous cases of tyranny!

Sheriff: Hah — yes; in the past, this humblest have passed some time in many places built by Iranian heretics; including that city of Ray and its outskirts. Truly, the victorious flag of religion has not ignored it. Yet if it weren't that this property of the Caliph of the Religion could not prosper without the serfs, in my opinion it would have been better to slaughter all these serf slaves to cleanse that ominous, befouled land with their blood.

Khurzâd: Your Fair Highness, you are galloping at full speed! Whatever silver and gold was in Iran was taken by force and brought to Baghdad, and all those handicrafts were melted and recast to glorify the steps of the Caliph and the nobles. Is it still not enough?

Mâhak: *[Agitated]* People live on dried whey and onion, and leek is like a luxury on their table! Didn't you see for yourself? There is no wisdom in Ray, as all the wise have escaped or migrated — what else do you want?

Sheriff: *[Bending his head]* You will know when need be!

Khurzâd: *[Terrified]* Oh, where is the one to turn the time and take us back with a wink to the ominous day we left Ray to come here to appeal; the tyranny in my homeland was better than this appealing in a far-off land!

Mâhak:	*[Terrified]* A cry — did you hear? Wasn't it he?
Khurzâd:	Fear has got me my sister — any cry sounds like his!
Sheriff:	These Iranians are a proud people. Be assured! That is a shameless man who is being taken all bloodied and in shackles. An atheist who has cast doubts on religion and betrayed the Caliph's trust! — I advise you strangers to have patience and calm, trust in God and prudence! Then you said that the original of that translation was this and nothing else!
Mâhak:	We came to ask but are being questioned again and again. Where's my brother? *[To Khurzâd]* Your husband — *[To the Sheriff]* who turned *Hezâr Afsân* into Arabic — and spent a thousand nights and days of his life on this! Did you not tell him "Finish this Arabic rendition in a thousand days, and I will reward you on the one thousand and first day?"
Khurzâd:	Don't lose your temper, my precious Mâhak! Calm down!
Mâhak:	*[Agitated]* Could he be calm? He was anxious to get the wage as nothing was left of all our haves and have-nots and no left-over remained on our table!
Khurzâd:	Don't say so much about hunger! Lest he thinks of us as beggars! We are in the house of the Head of Baghdad's Merchants, and he

is, of course, entitled to ask questions as he is also the Sheriff of Baghdad. Yet, despite all these, my astute master, be kind and tell us where my husband is; and where is that worthless wage which he was to receive for this translation?

Sheriff: *[Staring at Khurzâd]* Don't misunderstand; the mention of the wage was between me and him not you! It was between men — is that clear?

Mâhak: *[Shocked]* We are not here for begging — master! Aren't we guests of Baghdad with our hard work?

Khurzâd: *[Still confused, turns her head in fear and bitterness from the Sheriff's gaze]* Yes — I understand!

Sheriff: Wonderful! So you are in fact here for your husband who has disappeared since yesterday morning!

Khurzâd: Yes — my husband; who came to your house to submit and dedicate this grand work to you but did not return — *[Worried about Sheriff's ogling gaze, she turns her head quickly]* making my heart race, beating like drums.

Sheriff: By God, you are right to be worried — but as long as I'm the Sheriff of Baghdad there is by no means any reason to worry! Because — as reported — he is currently in the investigation room!

Khurzâd: *[Confused]* Interrogation room?

Sheriff: As a delegate of the grand warden, whose
             orders are to be obeyed, I will signal my people
             to inquire and investigate; and of course, we
             will soon have the news from the court.

             [He rises and goes out leisurely —]

Khurzâd: *[With a muffled roar from between her teeth]*
             Where are you Pour-e Farrokhân to see how
             pride is begging and generosity is pleading
             to beggars!

Sheriff: *[Closing both of the double door behind him]*
             Nothing else to say; go on your way.

             *[The two sides of the double door are red all over;
             with nails and hooks for hanging knives, daggers,
             saws, skewers, chisels, chains, tongs, pliers, whip,
             spear, shackles, and nail beds; and also the red,
             leather aprons of torturers. Mâhak rushes to the
             bucket, and hopelessly pulls out the ruined book —]*

Mâhak: I am really worried now. I swear by the God
             that is absent from the eyes, but not from
             the heart that I wish we had never come
             here to appeal for justice.

Khurzâd: And I wish my husband — your brother —
             had not, in his urge to support and provide
             for us, set his heart on these one thousand
             and one dinars, and had not translated
             Hezâr Afsân. I am worried about him in
             every joint of my body, feeling the agony in
             the marrow of my bones!

[Escaping from Mâhak's worried and questioning gaze, she gets away from her and walks towards her trade sack but remains midway as if taken by an idea or memory —]

— One day there was an dispute between a deceitful trader and a Zanzibari porter. When the policeman came, without a single question, he began to batter the Zanzibari, humiliating and insulting him while trampling his blood covered face to the ground — although he was the one telling the truth. This is how it is with the non-Arab tribute-payers. There is a difference between the conqueror and the conquered; and the Arabized Arabs and the ones they call serf slaves, the alien, Iranians!

Mâhak: You are worried about him, I about you; and he about both of us! How pale has become *Hezâr Afsân!*

Khurzâd: I know where to go and why shouldn't we go? To the grand warden — and his prison! There is an Iranian of Alavi sect, there, who has been kind to us — let's go and find him!

[The door is opened and closed. Now the curtain behind the door is also red. The man comes forward, wearing the cloths of the Iranian man —]

The Iranian: I will tell you whatever I have seen. No — how can I say it that you do not smell blood in my words! Come here — I have furtively written everything from behind the curtain!

[Giving a folded or rolled scroll to Khurzâd] What the prosecutor said — *[Giving a similar scroll to Mâhak]* and what the head of the police said! *[Controlling himself]* This dawn at the prayer time, your husband — Pour-e Farrokhân, Son of Mazdak-e Behdâd — took the translation to the Head of Merchants — the Sheriff of Baghdad — where in his presence the scribes went through it reading some passages, and the jurist and preacher questioned the content; each blaming him for something. The Grand Warden gave directives for formal investigation and asked for interrogators; and finally, after lashing and clubbing and shackling he was brought back, and the scribes smashed so many ink bottles on his head that he perished.

[The screams of the two women as they collapse and fall on the ground]

The Iranian: *[Remorseful, towards the sky]* Shouldn't I have said it?

Khurzâd: Ay, Ay, my man! Then in these one thousand days, you were drenching the pen in your own blood or painting the cloak of my fate with your black ink!

Mâhak: Though you received no wage, you are paying the wages of all these people, who gain their bread from your toil and agony!

Khurzâd: *[Roaring]* No, I can't believe it. As easily as that?

The Iranian: Why should I not say it and why should you not know? Come — it was here. *[He pulls out the rope from behind a chopping stump]* Your husband was in these shackles!

Khurzâd: *[Reading from the scroll]* You can choose between three forms of dying; we cut your wrist veins, put you in a sack and throw you into the Tigris, or strangle you after severing your tongue!

[Mâhak screams and Khurzâd hits herself on the head]

Mâhak: Now, I understand the sign! When my brother called you by your maiden name, he had lost hope in life!

Khurzâd: Yes, my precious Mâhak; for him showing *Hezâr Afsân* was the last hope for saving himself, but they washed it to hide the evidence!

The Iranian: May God forgive me for telling you the account of this interrogation. I, the helpless wretch that I am, was there as the only person among Sheriff's secretaries, who knows both languages.

Khurzâd: Oh — why did he ask me not to cry? Why did he set this condition! Why are my tears standing and my curses flowing?

Mâhak: Did they break his bones? Did blood spurt out of his throat? Did they cut out his eyes? Did they skin him and smash his fingers?

Khurzâd:	Did they crucify or maim him?
Mâhak:	What should we say to our relatives in Ray if still surviving under that tyrant! And how should we face those two back-bent dears whose harvest is taxed though their irrigation water is stopped? What shall we say after their long years of waiting?
The Iranian:	They are drumming and carrying the corpse. Come — they have spilled their share of blood today and are now counting their gains; don't stay here for a day longer! Put on men's clothing and get on your way to Ray!
Khurzâd:	*[Despondently]* Is Ray still where it was?
Mâhak:	*[Distracted]* Where is the single dinar to hire a camel or a boat? Or the food or means for the journey! Shall we become street prostitutes from hunger — and then be stoned to death by the curses of the foulmouthed?
Khurzâd:	No! — I shall know how he paid the penalty for his knowledge! So I will not ask myself why I did not ask about it today! Yes — I should know what came to pass!
The Iranian:	To know which people collected the reward for his blood?
Khurzâd:	To know how my homelessness came home!
The Iranian:	I am indebted to her husband; Oh God! What shall I do?
Mâhak:	*[Like deranged people]* I told him, brother, beware

not to drench this reed in your blood! He said, "This is a fountain spring from which each person drinks as much as their thirst!" I said, "Aren't there many who muddy the spring?"

The Iranian: *[Bringing the red aprons].* I know that by giving you these martyr accounts, I am being even crueller than they were. But come, you recite the prosecutor and you the head of the police.

Khurzâd: How can I be his executioner or torturer!

The Iranian: *[Giving each a red leather apron]* Have you not seen the passion play of Mani's martyrdom! Which the believers perform and each time he is revived with the performance?

Mâhak: *[Putting on the apron]* Let's revive him!

Khurzâd: *[Putting on the apron; while staring at the washed Hezâr Afsân]* Yes, I have heard that they set a table with a wide bench and cushions, and a chalice of milk; waiting all night, reciting the account of his martyrdom, and in the morning look at the milk and say that he was here — among us — as the milk has become less; and take the cracks on the chalice as his handprint and have wishes and divinations over them.

Mâhak: *[Taking the knives that the Iranian has brought; while staring at Hezâr Afsân]* What about us, two ill-fated outcasts, who have no table, chairs or milk!

Khurzâd: *[Showing her scroll]* We have his words. Come —

             *[She sharpens the knives that the Iranian gave
             her against one another. The Iranian puts on a
             torn and blood-stained shirt and hangs the scroll
             of his writing from his neck —]*

Mâhak: *[Sharpening the daggers against one another]*
             You should make yourself as cruel as the
             prosecutor!

Khurzâd: And you as rabid as the head of the police!

             *[Keeping their scrolls in their hands, the two
             women stamp their feet and roar. He picks up a
             rope which has been split into two from the
             middle and has metal rings at the two ends. He
             puts the rings on his wrists. The women kick the
             ground and roar —]*

The Iranian: Yes, they were as nasty as this! You should
             be bigmouthed, red-eyed and yell and yell! I
             am me, Pour-e Farrokhân, the scribe, son of
             Mazdak-e Behdâd! *[Puts a black sack on his
             head]* — you first!

Khurzâd: We will crush your mouth! Talk, you
             lowborn infidel! Which demon possessed
             you to turn this book from your alien tongue
             to Arabic and to insert the ideas of ancient
             Persians into Islamic accounts; and derail
             people away from their duty, obedience,
             faith, and the divine path and law — Ha?

The Iranian: God is my witness that your grandees asked
             me to translate this with kind words and

threats; a book that is worth reading and increases the wisdom of both the reader and the listener. But how and when did you slanderers reflect on and reach these wild and harsh accusations about a book that I presented to the sheriff this morning?

Khurzâd: *[Flustered]* I don't have the answer.

Mâhak: *[Stamps her foot]* The scholars of the Grand Library browsed through this elongated triviality and their word is our proof — yes — we believe in their decree, which finds faults in this from the "b" of beginning to the "d" of the end!

[She takes the bag off the Iranian's head. Light dazzles his eyes. Khurzâd holds up her spear]

The Iranian: I swear to the Great God of this universe that you had already decreed my immediate death before concocting these slanders. Or how is it possible that these people studied and mastered a book of this size with such a language on which I spent one thousand days and nights of my life? And this is not but due to your greed for those one thousand and one coins of Moroccan red gold, to which I will readily renounce my right here and now by the compassionate and merciful God. Let me go; my poor wife and sister have their eyes set on the door for my return, lonely and far from our homeland!

Mâhak: By the unforgiving, forceful God, we will not

get any rewards for killing you; and I am doing this work willingly for the Glory of God! This is the decree of the muftis on these ravings! Read — so you know what the faults are.

Khurzâd: The faults. Hah! This gibberish is all heresy and far from the tradition of the prophet! They have made this book to wreck our morals! Gobbledygook that creep into and ruins our faith! An account filled with superstition, false beliefs, and jumbled dreams! Women will take their jewel to the market after hearing it and the faithful will look away from their prayer mat! Of course, there is sweetness in it and it is not void of charm, but it is not appropriate for commoners who will freely sell their faith to desire. Perhaps, God protect us, it may be appropriate for His Highness, the Caliph, so his temper is cheered up; or for a minority of steadfast believers among the scholars and the elites and the grandees and the nobles who hold the rudder of reason in their competent hands.

The Iranian: Don't let your voice quiver and don't let that lump in your throat when you are playing the prosecutor!

Khurzâd: I am playing the prosecutor, whom I abhor. Speak, Pour-e Farrokhân, the scribe, or I will sew your lips!

The Iranian: I swear by the Compassionate and the Merciful God that your Sheriff asked me to do this with direct orders from your renowned nobles and grandees, insisting and urging me time after time. He quoted the elites who quoted the rulers of different regions, and the Sheriff himself had also heard it by his own ears that this book is the locus of the best of knowledge and thoughts, the true meeting place of heart and reason!

Mâhak: *[Pretends hitting him with the knife]* Cut this bragging, liar! If we don't stop you, you would say "the healing guide of this life and sufficient for the afterlife"!

Khurzâd: By God we know that all these riches would not have been added to ours if it had not been detracted from you, and this power would not have been multiplied to us if you had not been divided! Perhaps, with their bravery crushed, Iranians have decided to send forward this Shahrzâd to fight against us? Hah — yes; you, demon, brought this Shahrzâd to wage war against the fierce honour of the swordsmen of the warlike Caliph!

Mâhak: This book stinks of blasphemy and atheism! Replace the Caliph for "the King", and the Iranians' Damned Spirit for Shahrzâd, who treacherously uses these peculiar and far-fetched tales to distract the Caliph from admonishing, interrogating, punishing, subduing and killing, and make him reluctant to control and rule!

Khurzâd: You damned Iranians wanted to make the pillars of the Caliph's power obsessed with these rubbish words and false beliefs to distract them from the moral virtues and prayers of Islam and from conquering new lands and subduing more people with the overwhelming blade of us, the Arabs.

Mâhak: *[She pretends piercing him with a skewer]* Do you confess that you wrote this book in Arabic to cast cracks in the pillars of religion and corrupt the morals and manners of the people of the book?

The Iranian: *[Shouting in pain]* God knows you are set on murdering me and these are just excuses to spill my blood; otherwise, who does not know that this book was compiled in the bygone centuries, when neither you nor I lived! Where is the Head of Merchants — the Sheriff of Baghdad — who warranted this translation; and the grand warden to whom it had been read in Pahlavi when he was the governor of Fars and he was very eager to have it; and the far-sighted vizier who sent the caliph's messenger to encourage me to do the work more quickly?

Khurzâd: Why didn't you say how much obscenity is in this book and stupidity, and inanity and tales about indecent and vulgar people, why?

The Iranian: For me this book was all wisdom,

knowledge, foresight and brilliance. Where is the Sheriff of Baghdad who said the Caliph is looking for the tales of Iranian kings; and seeks among the relics of Roman Caesars and Iranian Kings a unique entertaining masterpiece befitting for his feasts; and he said this is a fresh and refreshing account remaining of the era of Iranian kings and worthy of his parties! And he promised me a thousand and one coins for the hardship of this translation, of which God knows I did not receive or see even one!

Mâhak: *[Piercing him with the skewer]* Ha, ha — we will tell your corpse about it as soon as we receive it! *[Crying] How could I not cry to become like the Head of the Police! [Shouting!]* By God, any form of death is less than what you deserve and any respite too long! For us one book is enough and that is the God's book!

Khurzâd: *[Taking out his knife]* By the god of Hira and Uhud who has no equals, you have challenged God's book, casting words onto words and tongue onto tongues and holding up your tales before the best of tales!

The Iranian: *[In pain]* I swear by the same God that you yourself asked me to do this hard job; otherwise, I had just come to Baghdad to complain of a tyrant governor who is whole-heartedly determined to destroy Ray! And I composed an ode in your tongue so that you would advise him to fairness and moderation.

Khurzâd: I am a worshiper of Al-Lat, Manât and Al-Uzza if I do not make you, Iranian, regret whining against an Arab governor! Who are you? Who allows you to plead to the Caliph against one of his governors? Don't even think of repeating this as my dagger thirstily craves for the blood of Iranians!

Mâhak: And the Knowing God of all tribes knows that you came to the City of Knowledge, Baghdad, because you foolishly assumed, like the other damned Iranians, that this is an Iranian city and has a Persian name; repeating their ravings and hogwash chitchats about "Bagh" being the name of your damned god and "dad" is Persian for "given by him"! And you're boasting that this is the city of God for whose expansion every brick was brought from Ctesiphon — aren't you?

Khurzâd: Being stupid and ignorant, your people say Shahrzâd's breath is the soul and mortar of these bricks as the builders and workers were every evening entertained with these tales in your old tongue to heal the wounds of their hearts and make them sleep better and forget their captivity!

Khurzâd & Mâhak: Say it — you came to Baghdad with the dream of seeing Ctesiphon.

The Iranian: *[In pain]* No — I came to Baghdad to plead for justice; but who will please justice for me? *[Sobbing]* Didn't the Sheriff say that the pure

Caliph is unable to fall asleep unless he can have the full *Hezâr Afsân* recited to him in Arabic? *[Getting angry]* He had heard from his vizier and he from his ambassadors, and he from many of the governors of Iranian lands that this book is the fountain of youth and light after darkness, release after tension and relief after hardship and grief, a huge architectural feat that is as much a palace of learning by example as the grand dome and terrace of Ctesiphon!

Khurzâd: Wow! If the Sheriff said that, I swear by the revenging God that you, being treacherous, did not translate *Hezâr Afsân*, but *[insinuating]* having promised it, concocted a book of your own accord to shake the pillars of religion and reason; which makes the spilling of your blood permissible. Where-where is the original of this book?

The Iranian: May God protect it from you and protect the ones who are preserving it!

Mâhak: *[Roaring, she takes out the skewer from the fire bucket]* I know how to deal with you if they can't find an original for this!

The Iranian: Water — I am thirsty!

Khurzâd: Don't bark, you, noisy dog, evil boar, infidel fabricator, speak — old hags telling stories and advising the Caliph! When did it happen and come to be, and which careful and reliable person ever heard and saw that women, even shrewd ones, surpass the men of the state in foresight? This is what you did with your translation of this unwelcome book to humiliate the best of Arab men. Why should a woman be able to say so many wise tales that even the oldest raconteurs of Baghdad fail to equal her!?

The Iranian: *[Weak and helpless]* Don't take her for less than she is, as I heard from my father, Mazdak-e Behdâd, who knows a lot about the ancient times, that she is not but an embodiment of the daughter of God, Ânâhitâ on earth, who has come for guiding the king; and is his leading companion to wisdom and justice! And isn't Shahrnâz, whose father Jam is the judge of afterlife, like this?

[Khurzâd and Mâhak caress his head and shoulder — while crying — and kiss the scroll hanging from his neck. Then, they both return to their roles —]

Mâhak: With all your malice and meanness, you just spoke some truth! Ha, ha! You delighted me with so many terrifying confessions! Now the suspicions of the library scholars about the mixing of Iranian beliefs with the God's tradition became certainty; and you did this to muddy the beliefs of common people!

Khurzâd: Is the woman a goddess that the ignorance of men drags down to earth? Is this the collective knowledge of Iranians?

The Iranian: Look for the meaning not the surface! And my father said that he had heard from astronomers that this is not but the story of the galaxy and the firmaments. Take the sun as the king, which shines and burns and falls sleep with the emergence and whispers of the moon, and the tales of the moon are our nightly dreams! Shahrzâd is the sleepless, night-wise moon that fades away in the day; and her sister that shadowy halo of air around her, there to support her; and the stars, are those that she rescues from burning in the fire of the sun. And if you do not understand this, you have never understood anything.

Khurzâd: Stop making up this gibberish and delivering your delirious thoughts! Are the jinns and giants and fairies and demons really going around or staying inside the faithful — from poor traders to diligent ascetics — as freely as it is said in this damned book?

The Iranian: *[Roaring]* Don't they? Aren't some of you the same jinns and giants and demons that live inside or among others — *[one of them pierces him with a skewer, and he shouts]* and you who use the authority of God to stab me with this skewer, aren't the faithful supposed to be brothers?

Mâhak: Prove you are one of the faithful.

The Iranian: If you are irritated by a brave, free woman,

and that she is the source of so much wisdom, and if you will be satisfied if I refute her; okay, I will refute her as my life is your hostage! *[Khurzâd and Mâhak are shocked!]* — yes by God, she could tell all these tales because two men helped her! The first being that murderous king who made her think of making stories to postpone her own death.

Mâhak: *[Ridiculing him]* Just like you, what you're doing — now?

The Iranian: And secondly, the compiler of this *Hezâr Afsân*, who gathered these stories from different regions of Indian, Roman, Arab, Egyptian, Zanzibari and Ethiopian lands, joined them together so the kings of the world know that there exists in the world many different people and ideas and do not rely just on their own opinions.

Khurzâd: *[Sneering]* Ha, ha — China, India, Rome, Arab lands, Egypt, Zanzibar, and Ethiopia — you foul-mouthed wretch say the lands of Iran; say from within the borders of the Iranian kings! From all these lands which belonged to Iran and are now under the blade of our intensity; and you are still craving them! Isn't that right?

Mâhak: And you bastard even deny God's daughter to save yourself?

The Iranian: Oh — water — I'm thirsty. By God, Shahrzâd

sought help and found it in words. I wish she would show me a way too; I am trying my best to save myself and can't find the way. *[Growling of pain]* Say any rubbish you want; cover the Iranians with sludge and yourself in gold; if you wish, take Shahrzâd's name off the book and replace her with one of your men; or burn the translation and scatter its ashes in the wind, but release me from this slaughterhouse!

Khurzâd: Burn the translation? Go to hell, you wretch; we beg for knowledge even in China!

The Iranian: Don't go too far; you are the world's teachers in injustice! Let me go, my wife and sister are anxiously waiting for me, desperate and empty-handed, alone in this land of atrocities; waiting for me to buy them some bread with the wage of this translation!

Mâhak: Rest in death, assured that they prefer water to quench the heat of their passionate desires! There are many customers for honey and sour-sweet nectar. Your sister and wife will have far better bread, and dates and butter, with their own commodity than what you can get them with these fabrications for which you are giving your life!

The Iranian: May God end your miserable lives or give you wisdom. Why this hatred? By God, what I did for you was the best anyone could do for you and the world —

Khurzâd:	Your job will be done only when we will have those two chaste women!
The Iranian:	You beat the drum of morality and the kettledrum of faith, but mock both. Damn you — if you don't want this translation, give it back and let me be!
Khurzâd:	You will be free only when you give us the details of this conspiracy, so we know if you, damned wretch, are alone in this plot or a group of Iranians are with you in this! The infidels set to ruin our religion out of spite and animosity are not few! Shall we pull out the tongue from your throat to make you speak?
The Iranian:	Don't cry; the prosecutor didn't cry; and don't beat yourself; he just beat him!
Mâhak:	Shall we rip your limbs one by one and throw them into the stove to make each confess your treason separately?
The Iranian:	By God, I am dying of thirst, give me some water!
Khurzâd:	You are free; to choose between three types of death; to cut your wrist veins after branding you, to put you in a bag and throw it into the Tigris, or to strangle you after pulling out your tongue!
The Iranian:	Is there no God in Baghdad that I can call with my cry?
Khurzâd:	The scholars of the Grand Library have jointly concluded that judging from the eloquence of

this translation, it cannot be the work of an Iranian; and the work of only one thousand days. It is the result of the collaboration of a group of eloquent scholars for at least ten years and with a planned purpose! Talk, who and where are your accessories, your accomplices in this conspiracy?

Mâhak: Shall we cut out your eyes from the sockets to make you see and expose the Iranians who assisted you in this conspiracy?

The Iranian: By God, I was lonelier than the God himself in this work!

Khurzâd: Are you claiming that you write Arabic more eloquently than the Arabs of Arab origin and the seven renowned geniuses?

The Iranian: Oh, all right — so it is jealousy nailing me on the cross; and greed making a purse for itself!

Mâhak: You, dying wretch; you don't even know the basic rules of conjugation and declension, let alone the rules of poetry and prose!

Khurzâd: Prove it by conjugating "to beat" or "to kill"!

The Iranian: By God, all our lives we have been conjugating "to beat" and "to kill"! What we never saw was someone conjugating to be just and to be fair![1]

Mâhak: Hah — if you don't know them, say their

---

1. "Zaraba/Daraba" (to beat), "qatala" (to kill), "adala" (to be just) and "nasafa" (to be fair).

	intensive forms or again if not that, say their transitive and intransitive forms!
The Iranian:	By God, I can say that a slanderer like you, the prosecutor, is not intransitive — but definitely transitive,[1] and an intensively vicious person,[2] like you, the Head of Police, is the best example of intensive form of over viciousness .
Khurzâd:	Don't make sarcastic and subtle remarks as the world will not be so subtle with you.
Mâhak:	Ha, ha! So we are now certain that you don't know Arabic!
Khurzâd:	And there hasn't been any one among the untruthful people of the past as unscrupulous as you, as you have mixed treason with spite and foulness. Yes — we have seen innumerable and unlimited signs and cases of intentional changes and heresies in your translation, infidel!
The Iranian:	I swear by the Glory of the All-Glorified God that I did not change anything in this; and anyone who knows Pahlavi, can confirm this by checking back with the original.
Khurzâd:	You deceitfully told the Sheriff that the origin of this book dates back to Zahhâk, but

---

1. Mote'adi means transitive in Arabic grammar and infringing and transgressive in its etymological sense.
2. "Sigheh-ye Mobâlegheh" (intense frequency adjective) has the sense of being intense and exaggerating.

we saw that there were no snakes on this king's shoulders!

The Iranian: This is a Zahhâk whose snakes cannot be seen. Yes — they have taken the snakes from the book because the snakes were specific to Zahhâk; but it was not just Zahhâk that had Zahhâk-like attitudes; Zahhâk-like people are on thrones everywhere. Zahhâk is still ruling with other names doing the same things!

Mâhak: *[Frightened]* Under the Caliph's name?

The Iranian: And you are his two snakes rabidly coiling around people to cut their brains out!

Khurzâd: Hah — my heart!

Mâhak: God, be my witness!

The Iranian: Indeed, this is my story; you arrest me for the sin of knowledge and want to kill me to take the brain for feeding your tyranny!

Khurzâd: *[Crying]* Where was God to stop his faithful followers from spilling the blood of the innocent! By God, he is delirious, and his tongue is not in his control!

Mâhak: *[Crying]* My darling Khurzâd — how could he take so much cursing and insult?

The Iranian: Don't cry over me if you're really the prosecutor and the Head of the Police!

Mâhak: *[Shouting]* Say, you Son of Auspicious, Son of

Jerjis, the Scribe of Ray — the ones saved by Shahrnâz are sword-wielding young men and the ones saved by Shahrzâd are virgins who may give birth to men! Why is that?

The Iranian: This distortion is not mine; it has come to be through the ages. Why can't Shahrnâz become Shahrzâd after two times one thousand and one years? And why can't Arnavâz become Dinâzâd after such a long time? And why can't Zahhâk, who suffered from his corporeal snakes, become a king who suffers due to the treachery of his better half? Yes, this was what the passage of time did — as this tale has been told differently according to the understanding of the people of each era. Thus, it is not strange that the emancipated are young men in one and young women in the other!

Mâhak: [Lashing him while crying] Is this due to your drunkenness, dreaminess, deceitfulness, or fake inventiveness?

The Iranian: Here I, Pour-e Farrokhân the Scribe, son of Mazdak-e Behdâd, will tell you that the first one is a tale of the age of epic, and the second is the tale of the age of reason, in which the sword is of no use!

Khurzâd: Heh! The age of your defeat — isn't it? Eloquence, and sweet-talk, and compliance. Ha, ha! Yes, flattery is the Iranian weapon!

The Iranian: Why so much lying? If you have ever learned to

be truthful, tell me why did you use all these tricks to get a book that you damn in public?

Khurzâd: If you don't know it, infidel, know now that with your death the scholars of the library will be free from any blame for having a hand in turning this book into Arabic! And if it contains any blasphemy, you will be the one punished for it in the day of doom. And now that with the will of God we have such a trophy in hand, our political wisdom requires that we use it to know more about fire-worshipping Iranians, who are nowadays among the conquered peoples of the Caliph's blade and under the shade of our shackles!

The Iranian: Oh — water!

Mâhak: *[To Khurzâd]* Put aside your deceit and duplicity! Why do you pretend it is for people's good? Why don't you confess? We have heard that there are love stories here about estrangement and reunion, and in some cases about the tricks of lovers and procuring ladies! *[Grabbing the Iranian by his collar]* Does it even make sense to fall in love with your executioner, have a baby with him and break the blade of his tyranny with that love? Is it really possible to make your executioner kind?

The Iranian: I am not the one who wrote this tale, unfortunately; I only went through a lot of pains to translate it, with no gains! But despite all these, yes — why not? If the person is Shahrzâd, why can't she transform the executioner?

Khurzâd: *[Roaring]* Does he mean us when he says executioner?

Mâhak: So ask those white-bodied beauties who are troubling your life to come here. Maybe your wife and sister make your executioners kind with their sweetness and cuteness. We have heard a lot about their beauty!

The Iranian: My wife and my sister are two noble *Âzâdeh* women, cypress trees, standing tall! May God's curse be on anyone who pester them!

Mâhak: What do you mean by *Âzâdeh*? You mean free-hearted and free?

Khurzâd: The state has coined new words for the free-hearted and free: prostitute and promiscuous. Understand?

Mâhak: Aren't we religiously required to provide custody and support for these beautiful bondwomen? The truely free-hearted are shackled!

The Iranian: Why live in a world, where the pen does not respect the hand that honoured it!

Khurzâd: Stop neighing and gargling vulgarities! You, materialist pagan, didn't you really know that we assigned police informers on your door? And that procuress, the owner of the inn, who was frequently sent to seduce them? Know that from the beginning till the end, you were being watched by the secret police. And the account of your two free-hearted beauties has gone house by house and district by district, and God knows how many of the grandees, nobles and officials have come to crave these two beauties and have been waiting for the end of this book! *[Worried]* Oh precious Mâhak — don't you remember the old hag, the owner of the inn, with her offers and tricks, asking us to sell ourselves to her eager buyers? And we — you and I — put up with the insult and did not tell your brother, so he would not worry and get distracted from this translation?

Mâhak: It doesn't surprise me if he gives up the ghost after this news! Don't you see he's standing on the gate of death unable to die for being worried about *[ridiculing]* his two free-hearted cypress trees?

Khurzâd: Speak Son of Auspicious, Son of Jerjis, what did you learn from this Shahrzâd?

The Iranian: *[With difficulty]* Everyone must learn how to speak under the blade!

Mâhak: *[Frightened, but as if she has caught him red-handed]* Like you — just now?

The Iranian: Anyone who trusts you! Shahrzâd knows that she will be alive as long as she tells tales!

Khurzâd: *[Crying]* You are speaking about yourself!

The Iranian: Yes — they have given her death, and she speaks of life!

Khurzâd: Say — Pour-e Farrokhân, the Son of Mazdak-e Behdâd — is this not but a nation under the blade of the executioner looking for a way to save itself?

Mâhak: I will trample each of his answers with my next question!

Khurzâd: No silence, man, answer!

Mâhak: What can he tell you if you are the prosecutor! Aw — My heart is in my mouth with worry. We must send a letter to the court to ask what to do with this *One Thousand and One Night*. Shall we tear it into pieces, burn it or destroy it with washing?

Khurzâd: Tear it into pieces or burn it? We are nothing but stupid if we do that. This translation is a war trophy taken from the infidels; and sharing war trophies is the sign of justice — especially because it has a lot of buyers among the grandees and nobles!

Mâhak: Yes — the account of this treasure of tales reached the Caliph years ago and he has been very eager to have it. And I heard from the Head of Merchants, who had heard it from the grand warden, and he from the grand ambassador, and he from the far-sighted vizier that today between the two prayers they had a discussion about the book in the court of the Caliph in which a verdict was reached — and sent to the head of the grand library — to distribute generous rewards in order to quickly wash the book of its Iranian vestiges, remove all the Magi customs; change the tales from the past to the present, and from Ctesiphon to Baghdad, and burn the original immediately!

Khurzâd: *[To the Iranian]* Hah! Did you hear, Son of Auspicious of Jerjis — no original remains! Is this still the tale of a people looking for a way to save itself under the blade of the executioner? *[Beating him]* Answer!

Mâhak: How could he say anything without breathing? He looks dead!

Khurzâd: *[Crying]* Ohh — so just like this? *[Sobbing and moaning while reading]* Who are these? These crazy Iranians who seek salvation in tales? — and he left this *One Thousand and One Nights* before death!

Mâhak: *[Roaring]* Don't die so soon, we are not finished yet, Son of Auspicious, Son of Jerjis, as just now according to our explicit orders you will be taken to the court of the Sheriff of Baghdad so that the scribes can confirm the findings of this interrogation by breaking their ink bottles on your head while cursing you! Oi! Where is this Iranian, go and call for a porter and a donkey-lender!

The Iranian: [*He unties himself*] Quickly, bring a stretcher!

Khurzâd: Ohhhhhh! — so this was the story of my ill-fated husband!

Mâhak: Ayyyyyy! — the story of my brother who left us in this world and leaped from it himself!

Khurzâd: He was among us or he is; as the water in this cup is less than it was.

The Iranian: Now you know everything.

Khurzâd: Oh — you, the cheap reed, you were nothing but a settler in the margins of the Euphrates; like so many that dry or burn on the roofs. Anyone made of you what was inside them. Why become the spear in the hand of one to torment and tyrannize the pen of the other?

Mâhak: No, you did not do this hard work as an easy gift for the hard-headed! You did this for the world!

Khurzâd: [*Taking the book*] Did you see how they kill the storyteller to sell the story at an extravagant price? You gave these tales to the world and became a tale that no one knows!

The Iranian: [*Anxious*] The night is falling.

Khurzâd: [*Throws down the ruined book*] The one thousand and first night.

The Iranian: Time to escape — as Pour-e Farrokh can only be alive in your words!

Khurzâd: Let me kiss the print of his hands on the chains!

Mâhak: The blood of his knees on this leg shackle!

The Iranian: Aaah! What is this sound? The Grand warden
            who used to be the governor of the ruined
            Ray! Beware of becoming captives! Don't let
            him see you! Escape or I will escape!

            *[He runs towards the door, goes out and closes
            the door behind him. The two women run, each to
            a different side, throwing the leather apron aside
            in fear]*

Mâhak: Shall we stay or run? I wish I could grow
            wings!

Khurzâd: I wish I could melt and go into the ground!

Mâhak: Death would be better than the Grand
            Warden!

Khurzâd: *[She starts to run, but halts and steps back]*
            Escape is escaping me. Where shall I go
            when my husband's blood is here?

Mâhak: My knees do not freeze and do not fail me!

Khurzâd: Ray is far; and where shall I go? What do I
            have?

Mâhak: Where shall I escape to — what shall I do
            with this report?

Khurzâd: Tear it into pieces, or eat it, or throw it into
            fire or water!

Mâhak: Why shall I die hungry? *[She eats the report]*

Khurzâd: Why shall I give away the Iranian guy to

death? *[She eats the report]*

[While chewing and kecking, they quickly put on their cloaks covering their head and body. The door opens. The Iranian is standing with the helmet and sword of the Grand Warden]

Grand Warden: I am the head of all prison guards; the grand warden! Which of you is Mâhak — his sister — and which Khurzâd-e Nikrokh?

Khurzâd: *[Covering herself]* I am Good-Looking, Daughter of the Sun!

Mâhak: *[Covering herself]* And I am Crescent!

Grand Warden: *[Violently]* Don't hide your tears, you, imposter hag! And you, weakling vixen! Don't gnash your teeth! *[Kindly]* It was heard and understood that you have come here to appeal and ask for Pour-e Farrokhân, Son of Mazdak-e Behdâd; your husband and your brother. It was not wrong; I can see that you are here. You must know that you are now two abandoned and frail women, and it has been decided that you had better be at the Caliph's court. It shall be clear to you that you Iranian women are the trophies of our war with that warring infidel whose corpse is being slapped right now.

[Khurzâd and Mâhak scream.]

Grand Warden: Patience is a vital religious virtue! I must make check this explicit order that I have just received to see what the exact requirements are. Shall I have you sent to the seraglio of the Caliph, to his secure and safe personal palace for recounting the tales of Shahrzâd, which you know well, or —

Mâhak: We and the Caliph? Instead of Shahrzâd and Dinâzâd?

Grand Warden: Or shall I give you to important officials; or directly sell you to the whorehouse?

Khurzâd: Like slaves or bondwomen? You didn't say how much and who will get the price?

Grand Warden: The Caliph passionately insisted on tasting the sweetness of these tales from your mouths; and would not have changed his mind if not for the reminding and advising of this humble servant and of course the Sheriff of Baghdad, who is one of his intimate companions, that, God forbid, you Iranians, due to your inherent prejudice and intrinsic arrogance may insert poisons in the words or vulgarities in the narration, and distress the Caliph!

Khurzâd: Recounting the tales of Shahrzâd — I don't believe it — my husband was murdered unjustly for the same reason. His body is still not buried!

Grand Warden: I won't be surprised if the earth rejects that corpse! But you may not know that the Caliph was enthralled with the accounts he had heard about *One Thousand and One Nights*. And I heard it from the far-sighted vizier — a most honest person — that he heard it by his own ears that the Caliph ordered to cleanse the book of its Iranian elements, insert Islamic thoughts and morals into it, make copies quickly for him, and wash the original in water.

[The two women silently turn their faces, and wearily sag on the floor each in a corner.]

Grand Warden: And I heard that he also said, "in this world and the other two books are enough for the Caliph of the God: the *Quran*, which is the book of celestial life on the shelf and mantelpiece; and *One Thousand and One Nights*, which is the book of this terrestrial life, under the cushions and close at hand". Heh — *[Taking out a letter]* And I heard that he said, "Let it be so, so that later the descendants of Iranians translate it from our tongue".

Khurzâd & Mâhak: *[Sighing]* Ahhh!

Grand Warden: *[Opening the letter]* Let me see what has been ordained in this noble letter. Mmm — Ha! Mâhak, uncover your face! You and your dazzling white beauty have been given to me, the Grand Warden.

Mâhak: *[Looking for a way to escape]* Aaaah, aww!

Grand Warden: I am enthralled with desire even if only half of what I have heard about your beauties is right! And Khurzâd-e Nikrokh — you, good-looking beauty, have been given to the impatient Sheriff of Baghdad who is eager to see your face!

Khurzâd: Aaaah, aww! — *[Escaping]* Ayayay!

Grand Warden: *[Emphasizing]* This verdict is ratified and conclusive, written by the pen and in the hand of the special scribe, and stamped with the stamp of His Highness, the Caliph of God, who has written: Good-looking, Daughter of the Sun and Crescent — the wife and the sister of that damned wretch — the account of whose goodness, understanding and beauty is on the tongues will be given specifically with the rights of their sale, possession, consummation, punishing and admonishing to the following: the former to the Sheriff of Baghdad and the latter to the Grand Warden. And the two are required to seek the satisfaction of the Lord of the World in obeying and pleasing their masters so that for the sake of the God's will — Iranians become few and the Arabs numerous!

Khurzâd: I want to say something.

Grand Warden: Nothing but goodbye!

Khurzâd: Just a few words —

Grand Warden: To contradict the Caliph's words?

Khurzâd: Don't separate us. It is hard in a foreign land.

Grand Warden: Separated, you will be more obedient!

Khurzâd: *[Helpless]* And maybe happier — *[To Mâhak]* at least, I won't see your embarrassment, and you mine!

Mâhak: I am glad I never had a husband to become a reward for his murderers!

Khurzâd: I am glad I never had a brother to pleasure his executioners with my body!

Grand Warden: I don't want to see any reluctance and refusal! Fighting against fate? Challenging your lot?

Khurzâd: Oh no — not at all — as the reign of the fate is in the hands of the Caliph; and one must give in, body and soul, to the desire of the Sheriff and the Grand Warden!

Grand Warden: Of course, you will consent!

Khurzâd: Of course! *[Hopelessly to Mâhak]* And this was the conclusion of our complaint against the unjust governor!

Mâhak: The end of this long hope!

Grand Warden: Just enough time for saying goodbye — *[He hammers the bell]* Ohy, bring palanquins and carriers —

Khurzâd: *[She goes towards Mâhak]* Don't separate from me now that my husband is not with me!

Mâhak: *[She goes towards Khurzâd]* Don't separate from me now that I do not have a brother!

Grand Warden: All done, goodbye! The servants of the Sheriff, bring your howdah, and my servants, set up the palanquin!

Mâhak: Goodbye Khurzâd-e Nikrokh!

Khurzâd: Goodbye Mâhak, Daughter of Mazdak-e Dabir!

[They put their hands under each other's cloaks and embrace each other, and suddenly strike each other with all their might. The Grand Warden, terrified and confused, reaches for his sword]

Grand Warden: What are you doing, you impure shrews!

[Mâhak and Khurzâd bring their hands out from under each other's cloaks, each with a bloody knife in one hand, holding the other hand on their heart. They walk back a step or two dizzily]

Khurzâd: We are free now!

Mâhak: We are free now!

Khurzâd: One day our complaint will be heard!

Mâhak: One day people will recount these injustices.

Khurzâd: That day you and I will revive!

Mâhak: *[She falls]* That day your name is Shahrzâd and mine, Dinâzâd!

Khurzâd: When the tale reached here, it was dawn and Shahrzâd stopped her tale!

[She also falls. The Grand Warden turns, confused and desperate, and the verdict falls from his hand on the ground!]

The
One Thousand and First Night
3

Characters:

Roshanak

Rokhsân

Mir Khân

The Stage:

A single summer bed is in the middle of the stage. Most of the objects and tools mentioned in the dialogue are not seen. Minimal background and as few objects and tools as possible! But the stage should suggest a five-windowed large room in a traditional Iranian house of the early 1910s.[1]

---

1. Panjdari is a large room with five arched double doors opening to a veranda or yard.

[Two sisters — Roshanak and Rokhsân — are conducting a ritual of death]

Roshanak: Come here sister — bring that indigo mat — or maybe the black one! Wail and put on a dark dress!

Rokhsân: Real mourning?

Roshanak: Don't you mourn if I die?

Rokhsân: I wish I am not alive to see the day. God forbid it! — but your husband may give up the ghost.

Roshanak: That will remain your dream, imagining men are so in love that they give up the ghost if we die.

Rokhsân: *[Unbelieving]* You mean he's not in love with you?

Roshanak: As much as he is in love with the bird he keeps in the cage!

Rokhsân: [Protesting] By God, you're unfair, sister!

Roshanak: And you're in love with your own
             daydreaming. Write: Give my bridal dues
             (Mehrieh) to the poor; and my dresses to no
             one but my sister.

Rokhsân: How should I write it when no one knows
             we know how to write?

Roshanak: Oh! I am such a fool! I forgot that we hide
             knowledge like the brand of infamy. My
             husband is pleased, assuming I only know as
             much as to deal with his trade accounts, and
             I do not reveal even that anywhere. Come
             here — how is light purple? Is it suitable for
             mourning?

Rokhsân: Everyone wears smoky black.

Roshanak: Not black! I am young — at least a shade, a
             bit of colour; some azure or green!

Rokhsân: Shall I cry?

Roshanak: As much as you can and from your heart!

Rokhsân: Isn't it hard?

Roshanak: Not as hard as dying itself! Sangria
             tablecloth and magenta shelf cloth — make
             everything indigo! Hand amulets on five
             sides; candles on six sides! Okay, now it is
             time to lie down. Where is the embroidered
             sheet? Come and help me spread it.

             [Rokhsân, perplexed and clumsy, brings the sheet]

Rokhsân:	How do you manage to hold your breath? And not burst into laughter?
Roshanak:	I will think about my own death; the death that will be mine one day; the death of my mother which is always before my eye; and the death of my grandmother, which was always before my mother's eyes.
Rokhsân:	Don't — I am already sobbing!
Roshanak:	I've been practising death for two years and nine months; since my wedding night. Upon his life, this is the test for a lesson that I have learned from life.
Rokhsân:	Don't scare me!
Roshanak:	Scatter straws on your head and tear your clothes! Scratch your cheeks and wail! You are my darling sister — who do I have except you?
Rokhsân:	No, wait! Not yet! *[Busying herself]* Wicker mat for women; cushion and hookah for men; hand fans for everyone!
Roshanak:	Why are you delaying me?
Rokhsân:	Soft halva, white sweet! Rosewater sprinklers in front of everyone. A tray of straw, here; a tray of ash, there! Light holders and lights on the upper corners and on the shelves!
Roshanak:	Rokhsân, I am talking to you!

Rokhsân:	For each cushion a rosary; and for each wicker mat a cup of mud!
Roshanak:	Worn-out coats for men!
Rokhsân:	Bowls of indigo for women!
Roshanak:	And some hired old women to scratch their faces and say sad words. Ask my husband how much he is ready to spend, to see if it is enough to hire criers?
Rokhsân:	Is it really necessary?
Roshanak:	Don't say you are scared!
Rokhsân:	I still don't have the heart, Roshanak; even to imagine it — but give me some time! Really — why did our mother set fire to herself?

[Roshanak pauses. She is upset!]

Roshanak:	May her soul rest in peace! She was my teacher. Despite her young age, she ran the school so efficiently that the mullahs who had schools hated her. A woman opening and running a school just opposite theirs, and little girls jumping around with happiness? This lion-handed, tiger-killing man of action — this Mir Khân — was the man assigned to carry out their religious decree for closing the school!
Rokhsân:	Oh! You never mentioned that!
Roshanak:	He was broad-shouldered and resolute. What a power! What an awesome scene, so

	many patrol guards and tough swordsmen, and the shine of their broadswords. You were just a child. You're still a child!
Rokhsân:	Say it — I can take it now!
Roshanak:	But the awesome scene vanished in the thin air, when in a blinking of an eye mother struck the match.
Rokhsân:	*[Breathless]* Oh — *[Roshanak steps away from her]* Please don't cry!
Roshanak:	The roughnecks, the heroes, heh, fled. The broadswords fell on the ground in panic. Cowed with the fear of death, the lionhearted burst into crying; and the religious ruling for closing the school burnt with her.
Rokhsân:	*[Complaining]* And despite all these you became his wife!
Roshanak:	Willingly. No one forced me.
Rokhsân:	*[Confused]* Really — I don't understand.
Roshanak:	Years later! We had both changed. Yes, changed. He was no longer that rebellious teenager, nor I that crying girl. He became bigger than he ever wanted to be, and I became beautiful!
Rokhsân:	You had many suitors!
Roshanak:	But I was waiting for him. From eleven to eighteen. I wanted him to know that I am from the same school.

Rokhsân:	Did he know?
Roshanak:	Soon he will!
Rokhsân:	*[Mocking]* Heh!
Roshanak:	My cheeks were on fire, and my heart raced! Don't you understand? Because of that ignorant man a fire lighted in my heart which still keeps me warm!
Rokhsân:	*[Obstinate]* By God, I will reject all my suitors, if I have any suitors, of course! I will shave my hair, rub mud on my head and lock myself up in a dungeon! *-[Upset and crying]*. Every match I strike —
Roshanak:	*[Shaking]* Every lamp I light —
Rokhsân:	Every stove —
Roshanak:	We left that neighbourhood; do you remember? And my father who died so young — he made book covers. He took us away from there, hoping to put out the fire in my delirious dreams; but I knew that every evening, he made a pilgrimage to that fire temple.
Rokhsân:	*[Rigid]* There are so many men; and better than him!
Roshanak:	You were not eleven, and you did not see him resolute, in action, all dressed up in armour and helmet with his sword!
Rokhsân:	*[Unbending]* Anyone but him!
Roshanak:	But he was the one assigned to carry out the

	verdict of closing the school; only him! Mir Khân; the best swordsman of the town! The owner of the earth and time; and deluded by other people's religious ruling!
Rokhsân:	*[Confused]* I don't understand you!
Roshanak:	Do you think others are better? Is there any man who has not burnt a woman?
Rokhsân:	Do you love him?
Roshanak:	Him, yes; his ignorance, no! *[Determined]* Change a man who is a role model for others. He is here. I can hear him! With his attendants and followers, orders and demands! — come, put this shroud that is adorned with words on me.
Rokhsân:	God's names?
Roshanak:	One Thousand and one!
Rokhsân:	Upon the holiness of writing which you taught me you no longer look like yourself!
Roshanak:	I always wanted to be like myself!
	[She sleeps on the bed and covers herself with a sheet.]
Mir Khân's Voice:	Servants and attendants remain ready at the door! The butler, the errand boy, and the chef start working. Tonight, we are having a feast as it is the night for dividing the profits!

[Rokhsân screams while marking her forehead with indigo.]

Intendant's Voice: The night for dealing with the books and accounts!

Attendant's Voice: The night for clearing the accounts!

[Rokhsân screams while tearing her cover into pieces!]

Intendant's Voice: The cry of mourning! Did you hear master?

[Rokhsân screams while scattering straws on her head. Mir Khân hastily comes inside, worried —]

Mir Khân: What's it! What's wrong? God forbid, you shriek as if you have heard the news of my death?

Rokhsân: *[Agitated]* I wish I'd die before saying it. Worse than that!

Mir Khân: Worse than the news of my death?

Rokhsân: *[Beating herself as if mourning]* The news of my sister's death.

Mir Khân: Never ever say that again! Haaa! Who's this lying here in the middle of the room — you ominous wretch! — my wife?

Rokhsân: Mir Khân, dear — ayay! Your mirror was broken, man of God. May Satan be deaf! May Satan be blind! You have lost your wife, man of God! *[Beating herself on the head]* Ayayay, God help us!

Mir Khân: *[Frightened]* Shut your mouth! Don't make

	me mad! Speak up, what happened, who are you talking about? Roshanak, my wife? *[Crying]* The one whom I was in love with a hundred times a day?
Rokhsân:	May God keep you; yes, my sister! The only person I have in the world. See, no sister in the world is as beautiful as she is!
Mir Khân:	*[He cannot bring himself to remove the sheet from Roshanak's face, agitated]* Is this her or her wronged soul?
Rokhsân:	Oh God! What had this champion done to deserve this, to lose his wife; and why didn't you take him?
Mir Khân:	Alas that fate is not open to bargains. No discounts, no delays! No threats and no bribes! Why's she dead and you alive? I wish you were in her place!
Rokhsân:	Or perhaps — your place!
Mir Khân:	Did you hold a mirror to check her breath, prick her with a needle, and slap her on the left and right?
Rokhsân:	Don't, with those heavy hands of yours, breaking —
Mir Khân:	My hand?
Rokhsân:	My dearest sister! See, you left him alone, despite all those claims of love!
Mir Khân:	Stop jabbering; let me have my grief in peace!

Rokhsân:	Do you think you are the only one; I'm grieving too and much more than you!
Mir Khân:	I don't even know whether you would really shut up or not if I strangled you?
Rokhsân:	Don't you know that I'll have even more grief if you strangle me?
Mir Khân:	It's not my fault that her time came before mine!
Rokhsân:	Search to see what evil you had done that this fire was cast on the house of your happiness!
Mir Khân:	You brat, don't say anything about fire!
Rokhsân:	[Ridiculing] You mean you don't even want the fire on your hookah?
Mir Khân:	May you become the fire-maker of hell, you fiery troublemaker — ooooh, I am reproaching you, but I am worse myself, burning in such a fire! Damn you, you are enjoying my suffering!
Rokhsân:	[Sarcastic] And how deeply you're suffering!
Mir Khân:	I'll die with her death!
Rokhsân:	Upon your life, I enjoy your suffering, but not at the cost of my darling sister's death who was like my mother! Oh, forgive me sister for trying your husband to see if he is really faithful to you, or not?
Roshanak:	[With a changed voice] And you know how I will deal with you if he is not faithful. I will kill you with my own hand after killing him!

Mir Khân:	*[Surprised]* Oh, the dead is speaking, what a miracle!
Rokhsân:	You underestimate my sister. *[To the dead]* I want to tell him to marry me, just to test him, sister!
Roshanak:	Oh, shut up, dear sister. If you ever try to seduce him, I will do something that the dead would weep for you!
Mir Khân:	*[Confused]* This is more than a miracle! She would not talk as much when she was alive!
Rokhsân:	Oho! You really think he is such a catch, don't you, my sister? *[Smiling, scared]* I know it is out of kindness that you would not let go of my skirt!
Roshanak:	Don't be sure! I am good for the mud if I don't drag you chatting brat down into mud!
Rokhsân:	Oh — help; the corpse would not let go of my skirt! *[To Mir Khân]* Don't you want to save me from her? Give a coin to the dead to let me go!
Mir Khân:	I will give her two coins to take you along! And I wish she would take me instead of you. With the death of my wife, all the women of the world are as good as dead to me.
Rokhsân:	Except for me, of course.
Roshanak:	Make an oath that you will not go near him after my death!

Rokhsân: How can I not when we are supposed to
             comfort each other after your death? Sister,
             you are joking with death in response to the
             joke death has played on —. What a power!
             Up to now we would not let go of the dead
             and now she would not let go of us — *[To Mir
             Khân]* Aren't you going to cut the dead's
             hand from my skirt?

Mir Khân: May my dagger be broken if I withhold from
             her what she wants! I am sure there is a
             prayer to recite for this!

Rokhsân: I know the prayer myself! *[To the dead]* If you
             don't let go, sister, I will have to take it off!

             *[Roshanak shouts furiously and lets go of the
             skirt! Mir Khân closes his eyes]*

Rokhsân: Oh, my sister, with your death the world will
             lose its beauty; water its fluidity and tree its
             greenness! Alas — see how she is awaiting
             death in her shroud.

Mir Khân: *[Crying]* No, don't rub salt on my wounds —
             [Confused] Awaiting death? *[Agitated, he runs
             towards the door]* Start beating basins to rout
             death! *[More confused]* Aw — awaiting death?
             My wife?

             [He pulls aside the sheet and steps back.]

Roshanak: *[With a changed voice]* You arrived in time my
             husband. I was fortunate to see you for the
             last time!

Mir Khân: *[Beating himself on the head]* The last time? —
Far from it! The last time?

Roshanak: It is a day that will finally come whatever we
do!

Rokhsân: God, take me sooner! *[Beating her chest]* I
wish I would die instead of you!

Mir Khân: Why you — when I am here? I who everyday
gave a coin to the poor for her health! Even
rocks will burst into tears if they know my
pain! Are there no words for my pain? What
would you say if your soul mate were dying
in front of your eyes, and you could not do
anything?

Rokhsân: *[As if working with an abacus]* I would say —
oh, what would come of my accounts?

Mir Khân: You, stupid —! My accounts? Yes, adding and
subtracting; multiplication and division! No —
wait; let me concentrate! *[Roaring, shows the
door to Rokhsân]* Tell the servants and
attendants to stay behind the door! To pray
and supplicate —

*[Rokhsân runs towards the door, crying and
beating herself on the head.]*

Mir Khân: *[Crying]* Did you say the last hour?
[Determined] No, I will spend everything, even
if it is one hundred coins to keep you alive —
even more! You're pale and have drops of
sweat on your face. Are you ill or unwell?

Roshanak: Be kind to me this last hour. Now that the hour of my death is approaching, and each beating of the pulse may be the last. *[She slowly gets up to a sitting position, with her own voice]* Ay — my darling. I have not yet been with you even for three springs. Will you ever remember me after I am gone?

Mir Khân: *[Agitated]* Oh, do not set my soul on fire!

[Rokhsân returns wailing and upset.]

Roshanak: I am really sorry my husband that your secretary and accountant are dying without your permission, and that at the same time and same place!

Mir Khân: They are not important, you are. You must remain alive.

Rokhsân: *[Beating herself]* Where and when are you going to find a wife who will be your secretary, your accountant, your housekeeper and your mistress? *[Remembering]* Of course, except for myself *[Quickly to avoid misunderstanding]*, whom you should never count on!

Mir Khân: What a brat! No — what can I say? These do not relieve the pain in my heart!

Rokhsân: *[Dancing with two Hukkahs in her hands]* Say oh — "what can I do without my secretary and accountant for each of whom I must pay big wages. How much should I pay the secretary to keep him reliable and how much to the

	accountant to stop him from embezzling my money; and what safety measures should I take to stop them from telling all the wolves and lambs about my haves and have-nots!
Mir Khân:	Why don't you say anything about this house which will be bleak and hollow without her? And the gaze of my emotions which will remain without their landscape? I want my wife!
Roshanak:	I am really sorry for all the money you gave to the poor for my sake; but my departure is out of my control. Instead, I promise I will die before you spent a hundred coins!
Mir Khân:	I said a thousand!
Rokhsân:	*[Challenging!]* What a liar! *[Beating her chest]* Oh my dear — my sister.
Roshanak:	*[With a changed voice]* But I know that I will remain in your memories; every night, when you get stuck in your accounts! Every night you miscount your number lines and hold the book of your belongings upside down.
Mir Khân:	Oh, do not sow salt on my wounds!
Roshanak:	Listen to my will, husband!
Mir Khân:	*[Crying — to Rokhsân]* Oh, no — I wish you knew how to write and would write her will!
Rokhsân:	*[Crying]* Or you yourself if it were not considered degrading to feudal lords' sons.

Mir Khân:	Shut up — *[Controlling himself. To Roshanak]* My ears are with you, my love!
Roshanak:	After my death, give the hand of my motherless sister to a husband who knows her worth!
Rokhsân:	*[Happy]* Wise, wealthy and well-informed — and not handsome? *[Upset]* Oh, sister, I expected more of you!
Roshanak:	A man with no horns, tails and hoofs; a man who will not beat her but is not an easily beaten underdog!
Mir Khân:	I will give special orders, tomorrow at the time of reviewing the cavalry, the first, best horseman.
Rokhsân:	Not a horseman; he may gallop away. I can at least catch him if he is from the infantry.
Roshanak:	I wish I could live to dance at your wedding.
Rokhsân:	Oh no, the bridegroom may faint of fear!
Mir Khân:	He will sure faint, but not for that, for seeing you in the bedroom!
Roshanak:	A man who will be her father, brother and husband!
Mir Khân:	How can I find such a fool, my dear!
Roshanak:	A man, who is an embodiment of manliness and an epitome of goodness.
Mir Khân:	These are all my descriptions!

Roshanak: A man who gives her a child better than himself!

Mir Khân: With these conditions I myself may have to become her serving slave — !

Rokhsân: *[Threatening]* Don't even think of setting your eyes on me!

Mir Khân: I will blind myself if I be such a fool!

Rokhsân: You don't seem to hate being one!

Roshanak: I know that you will find her such a man as soon as possible so she does not cling to you!

Mir Khân: I already pity him.

Rokhsân: Pity yourself who will remain with a craving heart!

Roshanak: A man whose soul and body are of equal weight, whose reason and heart are of equal power; whose bravery is not less than his forethought! Honest with everyone and with himself more than anyone else!

Rokhsân: Show me such a man, sister, and I will become her serving slave and clean the dust of his feet with my eyelashes.

Roshanak: A man whose head deserves to stay on his body.

Rokhsân: Does such a man really exist in the world?

Roshanak: A man who could fill my place for her, and the place of our departed father and mother.

Rokhsân:	Precious sister, don't list things that cannot be found!
Roshanak:	Yes, a man who is perfect!
Rokhsân:	Come on, I'm not so particular!
Mir Khân:	*[Agitated]* I can smell death in these last hour instructions.
Roshanak:	My mind is at peace about you, my husband, as I know you will find a wife better than me!
Mir Khân:	Don't say an impossible thing!
Rokhsân:	Why impossible when I am alive and around? And of course, impossible — as I won't become your wife!
Mir Khân:	I swear by God that after you I will forbid myself from all women! — I will slam shut the evil eyes and the bad mouth of any evil-wisher! Our town and land will be nothing but wasteland without you; and a wasteland will be the heart in my chest! *[Worried]* Tell me if you have a fever, a chill or an unknown illness? How are you so sure the hour of your death has come?
Roshanak:	I am as sure of it as I am of the coming of day after night and night after day!
Mir Khân:	No — no — no; Are you sure it's not one of those womanish absurdities!? As the wise say, two women are equal to one man in reason. Has a wiseman told you about your death?

Roshanak:	The wisest of all!
Mir Khân:	And the most honest?
Roshanak:	Someone who cannot have lied!
Mir Khân:	Who? A fortune-teller, a palm-reader, a deceitful physician, or an astrologer? God damn all of them! Who can know about their death ahead of time, when even the wise are clueless about their own tomorrows!
Rokhsân:	*[Mocking]* But apparently not about ours!
Mir Khân:	Okay; let's imagine the wisest of people has said it! How do we know he has told the truth?
Roshanak:	If even he has not told the truth, where should one look for truth in this world!?
Rokhsân:	*[Beating herself]* Ay, ay, ay! Alas, I lost my sister!
Mir Khân:	So a fortune-teller — or maybe a man — has given you this news?
Roshanak:	He is not closer to me than you are!
Mir Khân:	Thanks God a thousand times! A fortune-teller that you believe in?
Roshanak:	A man whose words I cannot dispute or contradict!
Mir Khân:	Who is this stupid scoundrel? Windbags tell a lot of lies for a few unworthy coins; which treacherous rascal is this? I'll break his neck!

Roshanak: Sheath your sword, and stop cursing, husband; that man is you yourself!

Mir Khân: Who? — *[stammering]* Di di di did you say who?

Roshanak: My husband, a man whose words I cannot dispute or contradict!

Rokhsân: *[Mocking uproar]* His well-being wrecked. His tongue stuck. Deathbed delirium. Oh, pity the man, pity him.

Mir Khân: What is this talk about death? What gibberish is this! Except the almighty God, who else in this wide world knows what tomorrow will bring?

Roshanak: You do, my husband. You know what tomorrow will bring!

Mir Khân: *[Confused!]* Me? *[To Rokhsân]* Did she say, me?

Roshanak: Yes, you did! And you can't have lied to me; and that on the first night of our marriage.

Mir Khân: I don't understand. Di di did I actually say that to you?

Rokhsân: *[Beating herself on the head]* She has gone mad, Mir Khân, do something, dear!

Roshanak: Yes, you said it yourself. Don't you remember?

Mir Khân: I — said such a thing?

[Roshanak starts walking like a ghost, slowly and like a shadow. Rokhsân and Mir Khân are baffled]

Roshanak: When I came to your house exactly two
              years and nine months ago, our wedding
              night! *[She stops]* There was a book in my
              dowry which belonged to my mother. Do
              you remember?

Mir Khân: *[Confused]* A book?

Rokhsân: *[Not following]* A Book?

Roshanak: In a velvet cover — which was dearer to me
              than my life as I had found it the same day
              among the little relics of my mother; and on
              its first page there was a sentence in her
              own writing, which said: "Wise is the one
              who reads this to the end!" And I found it
              blessing and blessed.

Mir Khân: *[Searching in his memories]* A book?

Roshanak: *One Thousand and One Nights*! Don't you
              remember?

Mir Khân: *[Frightened]* What? *[Taking out his broad sword
              and wielding it in the air]* Put on a prayer
              amulet and recite prayers for fending off
              jinn and demons. Don't ever mention the
              name of that book again!

              *[Rokhsân screams and starts making noises to
              fend off evil. Mir Khân draws a circle on the
              ground with the tip of his sword.]*

Mir Khân: As generation after generations our learned
              people have said, this is an ominous book
              with damning tales that distract young

women from the right path and older
women from obedience!

Rokhsân: [Frightened] One Thousand and One Nights?

Roshanak: Yes, husband; I had not even read a single
word of it.

Mir Khân: Better! That was why you were good! I
threw it away in the rubbish to be burnt for
the festival!

Roshanak: And I took it from the rubbish before
midnight and hid it somewhere.

Mir Khân: [Unbelieving] Did you really do that?

Roshanak: Just for that one sentence! I couldn't let you
burn my mother's handwriting! She was my
mother, not yours!

Mir Khân: Women should not read books. This is what
our learned people have said!

Rokhsân: Women should only keep their husbands'
accounts and books, don't you know that yet?

Roshanak: Yes, you said that, and I obeyed you; but you
also said something else.

Mir Khân: Whatever I said has come from our learned
people!

Roshanak: You said there is death in the pages of this
book; and any woman who reads this will
not get to the last night!

Mir Khân: Ahh, yes! — This is what our learned people

have said — that this is an ominous book; and an untimely death will be the fate of any woman who reads it.

Rokhsân: [Beating herself on the head] Alas my dear sister, alas!

Roshanak: You said such a woman will die before finishing the book, a painful, sudden death!

Mir Khân: What I said is the decree of our learned people.

Rokhsân: [Crying] Alas, Ayayay my darling — my sister!

Roshanak: So, death is in the pages of a book copied, bound and covered by my father? How can I doubt the sayings of the learned and my husband's words which are nothing but what the learned have said? It is two years and nine months that I have been waiting for my death every night!

Mir Khân: Haa?

Roshanak: At nights I added up your accounts and updated your property book, and during the day I read this book.

Mir Khân: [Not believing her!] Women's cunning! — Did you read One Thousand and One Nights?

Roshanak: I am at the threshold of death; why should I lie?

Mir Khân: [Angry] Did you read the tales that Shahrzâd told Shahryar?

Roshanak:	Shahrzâd was telling the tales to save her life; and I was reading with the hope of dying.
Rokhsân:	*[Interested]* Shahrzâd's tales were for sure better than keeping the accounts, weren't they?
Mir Khân:	When I read the first pages, I thought the work is done, the book of death had been leafed through and there was no returning.
Rokhsân:	Was that why you did not want to have a child?
Roshanak:	My children are my thoughts!
Mir Khân:	*[Roaring]* I wish they would be stillborn! Why should we ever need thoughts when the path of religion is before us? I wanted children who are of the same type as myself!
Roshanak:	Thoughtless children?
Mir Khân:	Living, as I am!
Roshanak:	*[Momentarily moving her hand toward her belly]* You will. A living child, alive due to thoughts as all my thoughts are for that child! *[Suddenly stopping herself from becoming emotional]* No — how can a dead person give birth to a living being? *[Keeping her balance with difficulty]* The poison of those words is still in my blood. The poison of the words that said any woman who reads this will die!
	[Rokhsân screams in fear.]
Mir Khân:	*[Baffled]* Motherless children!

Roshanak: *[Moving her hand to stop Rokhsân who is coming towards her]* You would also have died if you had read the book that I read!

Rokhsân: Where's that book, so I would not remain alive after you!

Roshanak: *[Smiling]* This could also be a tale from the same book! *[To Mir Khân]* You certainly have a face! And there is no woman who wants a faceless husband.

Mir Khân: *[Worried]* Call for physicians, prayer singers and criers! *[Almost Crying]* Her eyes have become blurry, haven't they? Doesn't she see my face?

Rokhsân: *[Teasing]* Or maybe she sees well!

Roshanak: You have a mask on!

Mir Khân: *[Angry]* What new things; a mask on my face?

Roshanak: Isn't the verdict of the learned a mask that you wear on your face to shun the burden of being yourself?

Mir Khân: *[Not following, to Rokhsân]* Did you hear?

Rokhsân: *[Shrugging]* Everybody is the mask they are wearing!

Roshanak: Not me! I wore the mask of obedience because you forced me to; and put it aside the moment that you turned your face!

Mir Khân: *[Shocked and unbelieving]* What did you do?

Roshanak:	And now I am tearing it into pieces before your eyes!
Mir Khân:	*[Breathless]* This is the doomsday!
Rokhsân:	*[Confused]* Have the dead come out of their graves?
Roshanak:	My greetings to her!
Mir Khân:	Women are trouble; but the learned have said, "May there be no house without trouble!"
Rokhsân:	Ha ha! How much learning is in this saying of the learned!
Mir Khân:	I wish this book had never been translated and printed in the royal printing house to make your father think of using his skills to decorate a copy of it with calligraphy, gilding and illustrations and leave it for you!
Roshanak:	And I wish he had lived much longer to teach me all those arts instead of taking them to his grave!
Rokhsân:	If having a husband is this, I prefer not to have one!
Mir Khân:	The learned say one must beat up such a woman or throw her into a dungeon or leave her for ever!
Rokhsân:	*[Crying]* As for now, she's the one leaving you.
Mir Khân:	Oh, no — the learned seem to be taking my life away from me! You, my wife — and the child that I do not know if you have, or you

don't have! My dear, at least you could have read the book and not told me!

Roshanak: Oh, my precious husband; please forgive me for my honesty; but I won't forgive you for teaching me to lie.

Mir Khân: *[Muddled]* What a paradise was my father's house! No books, no lessons; we were carefree and free. I never knew from among the six wives that my father had which was my mother, and it didn't really matter. There was a scribe who told us about prewritten fate and wrote letters; and an accountant who told us about the day of accounts and throw up updated accounts. Our minds were at ease, free from care. No one talked about the arts or troubled us with science! The only talks were of soldiers, markets, ceremonies and hunting; and of course, tales, and sometimes some from *One Thousand and One Nights*, but everyone knew it was only for men. How quickly those days passed!

Roshanak: After my death, return to your father's paradise, precious husband!

Mir Khân: *[Repulsed by the thought]* No — don't even talk about it! *[Pulling himself together]* Hah! — yes; they have decreed that pure eyes must not be cast on this book!

Roshanak: You had not said that they would insult you so badly every day by saying your eyes were

127

impure and you put up with it.

Mir Khân: Ha ha! Well, I'm not a woman!

Rokhsân: Thanks God, or you would remain husbandless, dear sister!

Roshanak: No need to worry, with so many loving men with pure eyes, I would definitely not die of loneliness!

Mir Khân: *[Agitated and awkward]* I did not say all men have pure eyes!

Rokhsân: I am offended. Do you mean my future husband will not have pure eyes?

Mir Khân: *[Impatient]* Meddling again!

Rokhsân: *[Angry]* Wayward troublemaker! I know what to do if I get hold of him!

Mir Khân: *[Mocking her]* in your dreams, of course!

Rokhsân: *[Fuming with rage]* I'm really mad!

Mir Khân: They are like this without reading books; what will happen if they do?

Rokhsân: *[Roaring]* My blood is boiling!

Mir Khân: Miss trouble, indeed. In any case, the learned have declared that this book will open women's ears and eyes to worldly matters!

Roshanak: You don't need to worry as I will soon close my eyes and ears for ever.

Rokhsân: Don't you think a woman whose eyes and

ears have remained closed to the world can more easily be tricked by a man whose eyes and ears have been fully opened.

Mir Khân: What? *[He angrily pushes Rokhsân away to stand in front of Roshanak]* Then every day you read one tale!

Roshanak: Every day. And every night I waited for my death!

Rokhsân: *[Pretends crying]* How you suffered, my sister. Your goodness reminds me of myself!

Roshanak: Every night I told myself "My death will be tonight!"; and in the morning when you went to the market and the storehouse, surprised and grateful for still being alive, I would hasten to take the book out from its cover in the chest that was itself in the small backroom behind the main cloakroom and enjoyed the taste of reading it!

Mir Khân: *[Maddened, he goes for his broad sword]* All those God-knows-what tales that I have heard from the storyteller?

Roshanak: If you've heard them, they were probably worth listening to.

Mir Khân: For men — so they beware of women's cunning! For women it is like poison dripping in drops! And death will be the fate of a woman who leafs through Shahrzâd's book!

Roshanak: Or maybe this death is what the learned

	wish for wise women! — and for suicide what is better than a book, whose reading summons death!
Mir Khân:	*[Stunned]* Why suicide?
Roshanak:	When I saw that from all that knowledge that I had learned from my father and mother you only wanted the adding and subtracting of your own accounts, my world was tightened, contracted. When I was deprived of the world in the four walls of your thoughts! When the world became as big as a grave for me, I told myself, why shouldn't I die? I leafed and read through Shahrzâd's book. Two years and nine months; and today I read the last pages, to the last words! And I said, "It's a wonder, if I haven't died till today, then my death will come today".
Rokhsân:	*[Crying and beating herself on the chest]* Don't say that — don't die — don't leave me with no sisters.
Roshanak:	The book was read to the end. If I don't die, you have all lied; and I will ask why!
Mir Khân:	*[Looking at his hands]* If you don't die!
Rokhsân:	Keep alive — as you would expose a big lie with your life!
Roshanak:	Why should my husband have lied to me?
Mir Khân:	*[Hoping]* Or you're lying; and you haven't read anything from that book!

Roshanak:	Which of the tales would you like to hear? The tales of the merchants? Those of the animals? Those of the lovers? Or those of the jinnis and fairies?
Mir Khân:	Or the one about women's cunning?
Roshanak:	Wisdom is called cunning when it comes to women! And cunning is called reason when it comes to men!
Mir Khân:	There are also tales about shameless women!
Roshanak:	Who are the results of shameless men!
Mir Khân:	And about bondsmen and bondwomen!
Roshanak:	Who are more gifted than their masters!
Mir Khân:	And about slaves!
Roshanak:	Who reach freedom!
Mir Khân:	Then you've read all of them!
Roshanak:	I love the tale of the woman who sat behind a reed panel and healed people.

[Mir Khân reaches for his broadsword.]

Rokhsân:	*[Screaming]* Here comes death!
Mir Khân:	*[Raising his sword]* Tell him to hurry up!
Roshanak:	And you sweep the path for death! *[Mir Khân remains hesitant]* This is a unique house, easily seen, outstanding, with a straight address. In the turn of which small alley is

	death lost, panting?
Mir Khân:	*[Baffled]* Then you've read all of them!
Roshanak:	And that's why I'm content to die!
Rokhsân:	Aw, my sister — I wish I too had read the book and would die with you!
Roshanak:	Reading is my legacy for you. Give my bridal dues to the poor; and the dress I'm wearing only to my sister!
Mir Khân:	I can't wish for your death, but this is too much for me. Then you, you have read all of them!
Roshanak:	Even more than that; I've also written things — for others to read.
Mir Khân:	*[Baffled]* You — have written?
Roshanak:	Tales that Shahrzâd didn't tell!

[The broadsword falls from Mir Khân's hand. Pause. Baffled and muddled, he turns and walks away from Roshanak.]

| Mir Khân: | Our learned people lied. You're wise. From this book you learned how to live. Why should I say otherwise? This is the magic breath of Shahrzâd that the storyteller told us about! And all this time I remained what I was. A man who talks of the wisdom of the learned and not of his own wisdom. A man who is incapable of dealing with his own accounts; and has heard Shahrzâd's tales only through storytellers! Put aside the |

	mourning stuff; and instead teach me literacy. I want to read books.
	[Rokhsân goes forward to take the shroud off Roshanak.]
Rokhsân:	*[Surprised by the outcome]* If you don't die my sister, oh, this will be your rebirth!
Roshanak:	*[To Mir Khân]* And why shouldn't it be your rebirth? Give me the key to the school building. My mother is there under a stone, sleeping in her ashes. Let's go and light up her light; with the same fire in which she burned!
Mir Khân:	*[Confused]* Did you know that woman? The woman who never vanished from my dreams? The woman who still, every night, screams in the fire of my dreams?
Roshanak:	She screams because by closing the school, you burned all those girls who could learn things all these years.
Mir Khân:	*[Baffled]* I always asked myself where I had seen those eyes. Then you were there!
Roshanak:	I am the pupil of the same school!
Rokhsân:	*[Lighting the light]* The burning coal under the same ashes!
Roshanak:	And the daughter of the same mother!
Mir Khân:	I shall put aside my sword as your victory came with no swords! Tomorrow we will clean the school; and you're a good teacher,

133

Shahrzâd, as you teach without censuring! *[Calling to outside]* Is there no one to pick a bunch of flowers — to celebrate the happy elimination of disaster? *[He sends Rokhsân ahead]* Tell the servants and attendants to sing happy songs! Let happiness come now that death is gone!

[Rokhsân runs out and quickly opens the door, screaming with happiness and scatters a handful of sweets in the air and hooraying; sounds of happy hooraying from outside. Mir Khân goes towards the door, making an announcement while throwing coins into the yard —]

Mir Khân: Tonight, we will have a feast as it's the night of accounts; the night of clearing the debts; the night of dividing the profits!

Roshanak: *[Taking a step ahead, while moving her hand towards her heart]* The one thousand and first night!

The End.

Continuity and Resistance through Emancipatory Speech: The Story of a Book.

Introduction: A Book and A Myth

The One Thousand and First Night is a play about the origins and the history of a book called *Hezâr Afsân* (A Thousand Tales), which following its translation into Arabic in the eighth century and its vanishing in the eleventh century, has come to be known as *One Thousand and One Night*.[1] The play, however, is equally rooted in Beyzaie's interest in the origins of the idea of emancipatory speech, performance and action, its evolution in epics, romances and folktales, and its importance as a locus for marking female agency in action against toxic masculinity.

The link between these two fields is that the central trope in the cultural products associated with emancipatory speech, performance and action involves the cooperation or the conflict of two creative figures in a process in which the knowledge, divergent thinking and artistic skills of one or both of them transform a violent ruler to a benevolent role model and source of prosperity, or, if that is not possible, distract him and engineer his downfall. The motif, which is observed in carnival, folktale, historical or epic

---

[1] For references to *Hezâr Afsân*, see Ibn-e Nadim, *Fihrist*, Chapter 8, 712-15 (Arabic 321-22) (Persian 538-41); and Mas'udi, Morravej al-Zahab (*Moravvej-oz-Zahab*), 610-11.

forms, has its origins in agricultural myths associated with the rituals conducted to guarantee the rebirth of nature after its annual death in winter and its later evolution into the myths about heroes slaying dragons and demons.[1] In my article below, I will explore the transformations of these tropes in Beyzaie's works to ground my analysis of *The One Thousand and First Night*. To highlight the emancipatory import of Beyzaie's approach, I will also discuss the historical givens of the time of annunciation in the context of women's movement and people's resistance against the state's violent bid for the Islamification of the culture after the revolution which led to the marginalization of significant secular aspects of Iran's traditional and modern culture.

Background: Origins and Rise of an Emancipatory Discourse

Beyzaie's fascination with the trope of female emancipatory action originates in the folktale of "Mehrin Negâr and the Snake King" which his grandmother recounted for him in childhood.[2] In the tale, which has correspondences with the universal categories of ATU425A and B (Snake Spouse Tales) and ATU433C (Search for the Lost Husband), a young woman, Mehrin Negâr is forced to marry a snake king, realizes he is a handsome prince, burns his snake mask, and, when he vanishes, sets off to find him in the land of demons where he is trapped by his demonic foster mother. She is forced to fulfil tasks set by her mother-in-law and ultimately escapes with the prince. Negâr's emancipatory action in the tale has two aspects: (1) she burns the mask of toxic masculinity to release the man inside, and (2) embarks on a quest to the underworld of demons to reclaim his beloved and use his tremendous force and acumen for prosperity.

The tale has correspondences with other tales which include a journey to the underworld or an encounter with death to save a beloved, including the Indian tale of "Savitri and Satyavan". It is also like the Greek tale of "Psyche and Cupid", but due to the Zoroastrian reshuffling of the Indo-European pantheons, Cupid's mother, Aphrodite, a goddess in the Greek tale, is a *dīv* (demon) in

---

1. See Frazer, Golden Bough, "Book II: Killing the God", 223-556.
2. Beyzaie, "Ostureh-hâ"

the Iranian tale. The girl's name, however, also associates her with Mithrâ/Ânâhitâ, who are Sun/Water animist deities in Iranian agricultural myths. The snake imagery also signifies a link with the earth in a plot focused on whether the male principle penetrating the earth (the snake) can be used to fulfil the earth's ideal of fertility and prosperity, or it remains imprisoned in toxic masculinity which prides itself in destroying and killing rather than planting, raising, and protecting. The essence of the tale, therefore, also has correspondences with the myth of Ishtar and Tammuz in which Ishtar, the Mesopotamian goddess of love, fertility, beauty, sex, and — for defending the former — war, justice, and political power, travels to the underworld to save her beloved agent of fertility, Tammuz from her sister Ereshkigal, the queen of the netherworld. More important, however, are the links with the myth of the dragon king Zahhâk who is to be slayed as he is incorrigible and the framing story of *One Thousand and One Night* in which the two sisters, Shahrzâd and Dinâzâd liberate the man from his mask of toxic masculinity and make him serve the ideals of fertility and prosperity.

Beyzaie reworked this folktale in his emancipatory play *The Snake King* (1966), in which Negâr and the Snake King, ideal leaders, transform the demons, the downtrodden, into citizens, unite them against a usurping centre, and liberate the country before relinquishing power to open the path for democratic change. He also expanded its motifs to create two quest templates that are usually used for men: (1) women as questing saviours akin to the legends of Rostam, Gīv, Perseus, and other male heroes, and (2) women as civilizers in line with the function of wisemen in legends such as Ermâeil and Gaermâeil, Zâl or Bozorgmehr in *The Shahnameh*, or the later Iranian intellectuals and premiers who aspired to be like these heroes or were seen as such by the posterity due to their role in reforming internal tyrants or foreign invaders. Beyzaie, thus, introduced two creative paths for depicting women as initiators of change.

This initiative implies a concern with gender equality but considering the cinema's obsession with mixing the motifs of toxic masculinity with those of male heroism, I argue that he has been equally concerned with subverting the culture of toxic masculinity which the economic, political, religious and cultural centres use to promote their coercive monologues and supress unwanted practices by symbolic and physical violence. This toxic culture which is also echoed in toxic femineity is primarily preserved by men's desire to obtain qualities that, they assume, prove their masculinity and women who are conditioned to desire such types of masculinity. That is why Beyzaie's ideal women, as seen in *Downpour, Stranger and the Fog, Ballad of Târâ* or *Bashu, the Little Stranger*, ultimately desire men who can create, construct, and protect rather than destroy. Thus, Beyzaie's heroines act as role models for women not just for the sake of women but also for the roles such women can play in subverting the vicious circle of female desire and male aspiration that produces toxic masculinity.

Moreover, though they engage in quests, Beyzaie's heroines are far from the distorted image of warrior women in Iranian romances such as *Samak Ayyâr* or recent Hollywood films in which tough women play the same absurdly violent roles that their male counterparts play. They are, thus, closer to the archetypes of wise civilizers. In its Iranian context, this intellectual template has evolved to mythologize the civilizing roles of Iranian premiers and intellectuals whose deeds are deemed influential in preserving the idea of Iran and controlling the violence of internal or invading rulers. The roles played by women in such practices, however, have remained limited to folktales. In Beyzaie's works, however, like their male equals, they represent emancipating action, speech and performance. Thus, at an archetypal level, they function like the priests or priestess in fertility rituals, whose words and actions were to contain the demons of draught, direct the forces of nature into channels of fertility and set the stage for the return or rise of the dying vegetation god or fertility hero. Though Beyzaie's research on the subject in *Where is Hezâr Afsân?* and its creative portrayal in *The One Thousand and First Night* are focused on the neglected roles of women, in his other works such as *New Preface to the Shahnameh* (1986), *Parchment of Master Sharzin* (1986) and *Account of Bondar the Premier* (1961/1995), he depicts the sacrificial contribution of creative intellectuals to reforming their culture.[1]

---

[1] For more, see Talajooy, "Reformulation" and "Intellectuals".

The existence of these emancipatory male or female roles makes perfect sense, as the civilizing or controlling roles attributed to the premiers or intellectuals may also have been fulfilled by those women who married violent rulers and whispered wisdom into their ears or having given birth to their children cooperated with premiers and their children's teachers to turn the next dynastic generation into patrons of arts and protectors of people. These are, of course, idealized reconstructions of actual circumstances in which invaders used marriage with local dignitaries' daughters and the influence of their intellectuals or religious leaders to gain legitimacy and guarantee the continuity of their rule. The process also always meant that even when these women or intellectuals did join the victors with the hope of changing them, they may have changed as much in the process as the rulers that they tried to change or as in the case of Nizam-al-Mulk (1018-92), the renowned premier of Alp Arsalan (r. 1063-74) and Malek Shah I (r. 1072-92), they fulfilled their plans for stability and prosperity by suppressing alternative views.[1] Thus, wives may have acted cruelly to make their children crown prince, or premiers may have committed atrocities to keep their positions or fulfil utopian illusions.

Regardless of the actual cases, however, whereas the contributions of male intellectuals to the country's prosperity have been celebrated in literature, history and folklore, the roles of women have mostly survived in folk narratives. The two have also generated two distinct paths, which have found their ideal examples in (1) the Cycle of Zahhâk where two learned men act as agents of emancipation by a cooking stratagem, and (2) the framing story of *A Thousand Tales* in which two sisters, Shahrzâd and Dinâzâd act as agents of emancipation by performances in which one plays the recounter and the other the listener.[2] In his research, Beyzaie links these two narratives to several others, highlights the emancipatory roles of two women in them, and identifies the agricultural origins of such narratives by associating the sisters with the spirit of earth and water and their cooperation in their own

---

[1] For his ideas about political stability, see Nizam al-Mulk, *Siyâsatnâmeh* (*Siyasat-nama*), Chapters 44-47.
[2] See Beyzaie, *Risheh-yâbi*; and *Hezâr Afsân*, 75-126.

and their people's liberation. I argue that the similarity of the two narratives is also reflected in the names of their protagonists. In the cycle of Zahhâk, the epithet of Ermâeil (Armânak/Irmân) is *pâkdin* (of pious/true religion), which links him to religion and that of Gaermâeil (Garmânak/Gaoirmân) is *pishbin* (of foresight), which links him to political wisdom.[1] Interestingly, the heroines' names in the framing story of *A Thousand Tales* reflect similar qualities. Dinâzâd's name means of free and true religion and Shahrzâd's name reflects Shahrâzâd which has to do with politics as it means a free city. In Zahhâk's myth, the dragon king must feed the brains of two young men to his snakes every night, but Ermâeil and Gaermâeil find a way to save one man every night. In *A Thousand Tales*, Shahryâr marries a virgin every night and has her executed in the morning, but the two sisters reform him into a hero of prosperity as implied in his name and his attitudes before he turned into a dragon due to his first wife's betrayal. In the former, which is concerned with epic heroism and liberating the homeland through conquest, the saviours and the saved are men. In the latter, which is a folktale and thus transmitted more by women and concerned, among other things, with survival under patriarchal tyranny, the saviours and the saved are female. Both, however, are primarily concerned with annulling the threats that Zahhâk and Shahryâr are posing to the country's generational continuity and fertility by slaying young men and women.

Beyzaie highlights the agricultural origins of both and analyses the mythologization process that has combined different events to produce the two narratives. He also suggests a shared origin by suggesting that those who engineered the plot of saving the men from Zahhâk's snakes were Jamshid's daughters. I agree with these points and Beyzaie's points about the two sisters representing the Goddesses of earth (Spandârmaz) and waters (Ânâhitâ). However, I also argue that at an archetypal level Armânak and Garmânak represent the priests of these goddesses and at the legend's socio-political level, they represent the cultural and political intellectuals that supported Jamshid's daughters, the rightful leaders, in the process.

---

[1] Beyzaie (*Hezâr*, 152-4) offers a convincing analysis of their names, but does not focus on their epithets.

In a little studied narrative about Spandârmaz, the goddess, whose name suggests "ripeness of mind" and "intelligence", appears to Manuchehr, the Iranian just ruler to guide him and his craftsmen on how to make a special bow and arrow and then summons Ârash to shoot the arrow that flies from Damavand Mount to the Oxus rivers and liberates Irânshahr from Afrâsiyâb's bondage.[1] This is interesting as, according to another myth, prior to her liberation "the earth [Spandârmaz] was a virgin betrothed" to Afrâsiyâb whose name signifies "the suppression of waters, draining of rivers, and causing of drought, famine, and desolation".[2] Spandârmaz's association with female agency can also be seen in *Mardgirân* (Getting a man) or *Mozhdgirân* (Getting gifts) ritual, performed during the Feast of Spandârmaz, in which wives received gifts from their husbands, and virgins were allowed to choose their husbands.[3] Thus, Spandârmaz, the ideal strategist who chooses her own husband and turns him into the saviour of the land is represented in the play in Shahrnâz of the *Shahnameh* and Shahrzâd of the *One Thousand and One Night*; and Ânâhitâ, the divine protectress of waters and guarantor of the victory of heroes of fertility is depicted as Arnavâz of the *Shahnameh* and Dinâzâd of *A Thousand Tale*. One may, therefore, argue that in the original myths, women who represented these goddesses assisted their intellectual supporters and heroes of fertility, and the intellectual supporters and heroes supported these women. Yet whereas in *A Thousand Tale*, Shahrzâd's father, her intellectual supporter, has no agency, in the *Shahnameh*, the two sisters have no agency. In one the goddesses, themselves are given centrality, in the other, their priests.

A Play of Survival in Three Parts

The play, however, goes beyond identifying the mythical origins of the book to examine the possibility of emancipatory speech in three contexts which suggest the continuity of forces of

---

[1] Biruni, *Al-Âthâr*, 334-35 (English 205-06). The English translator assumes Spandârmaz is a male figure.

[2] Yarshater, "AFRÂSĪÂB". Boyce, History 1, 206; Skjærvø, "Ahura Mazdâ", 404-09.

[3] Biruni, *Al-Âthâr*, 355, (English 216); and Gardizi, *Zein-ol-Akhbâr*, 237.

destruction and construction in contemporary life and the roles played by constructive men and women in society, particularly those women who carry the emblem of intellectual and cultural survival when their male counterparts have been already slayed. In other words, in addition to tracing the history of a book and celebrating women's agency, it also highlights the continual rebirths of the idea of Iran as a thriving culture despite internal and external tyranny. Thus, it also contains linguistic and stylistic features that echo Iran's cultural transitions.

The first part, as suggested above, suggests a shared origin for the myth of Zahhâk and the framing story of *One Thousand and One Night* and depicts Shahrnâz and Arnavâz as agents of liberation. They employ two chefs, set up the plot that enables them to save one young man every day, and recount and perform tales to distract Zahhâk and his snakes from realizing that one of the brains they are fed with is a sheep's. The second part is set in the early Islamic era, when after having the book translated into Arabic, the Sheriff of Baghdad destroys its only extant Middle Persian copy by placing it into a bucket of water. Eager to prove the superiority of their culture and possessing the translator's wife and sister, he and his cohort, then, get the clergy to declare the translator a heretic and torture him to death for trying to corrupt Moslems by mixing Zoroastrian ideas with Islamic ones. The events of the translator's death are enacted in *ta'ziyeh-like* performance by an Iranian scribe, and the translator's wife and sister before the two women undergo ritual self-annihilation to avoid being turned into sexual toys for the ruling elite. The final part, then, flash forward by a thousand years to a few decades after the book has been translated back into Persian. An educated woman initiates a plan in which she marries the influential head of a pressure group against women's literacy, pretends to have died of reading *One Thousand and One Nights* in anticipation of what clerics have declared about women who dare to read the book, and manages to reform him with her sister's help.

Thus, in the first part of the play, the sisters fail to reform the dragon but save young men to prepare the path for a revolution. In the second, the two women fail to reform the rulers or save their brother but avoid sexual slavery by undergoing ritual suicide. In the third, they set up a performance that reforms an epitome of toxic masculinity and suppressive religiosity. The styles of the three plays echo their settings and subjects. The first is in pure Persian to reflect the language of pre-Islamic Iran and is dramatized in a *naqqâli* recitation style with epic, carnivalesque and *taqlid* elements that link it to *One Thousand and One Night* and the *Shahnameh*. The second is written in a *ta'ziyeh*-like passion play style, in which three gifted individuals, a man and two women, are depicted as sacrificial heroes and the Arabic-ridden discourse of the rulers of eighth century Iran is set against the protagonists' Persian. Working with the same premises, the third play is an improvisatory *taqlid* comedy in a language that echoes the intricacies of women's idiomatic speech and typical aphorisms, yarns, jokes, songs and games in the first decade of the twentieth century.

Beyzaie wrote the third part first for a festival entitled *1001 Nights-Today* in Denmark, where it was staged by Alan Lyddiard at The Betty Nansen Theatre, Copenhagen, on 30 December 2002. He, then, went on and completed the rest and staged the play in Tehran in autumn 2003.

Part One:

"The play's the thing to uncover the conscience of the king"[1]

One of the emancipatory elements in Beyzaie's dramaturgy is his use of self-reflexive motifs, particularly dramatic rituals and plays within a main play in contexts that set conflicting discourses against one another and mark human identity as a multi-layered set of performances for the self itself and the other. The process also reframes a key feature of Iranian plays in which each character/actor may play several roles and step in and out of these roles to display their personal feelings by talking to the audience or creating other forms of actor-spectator links with fictional audiences in and actual ones outside the play. His plays also often juxtapose the unities of time, action, and place with the Iranian plays' use of free movement in time and space by subplots that expand the time, space, and action without breaking the play's overall unity.[2] Thus, whereas Hamlet uses his play as a ruse to

---

1. Shakespeare, *Hamlet*, Act 2, Scene 2.
2. For more see, Talajooy, *History*.

"uncover the conscience of the king", Shahrnâz and Arnavâz use theirs to distract him while saving people and organizing a revolution.

In the play, Shahrnâz and Arnavâz, in line with their intellectual flexibility and creativity, play several roles for the audience and for Zahhâk as a participating spectator within the play. Among other things, this role playing suggests how Zahhâk's self-obsession makes him unable to imagine himself as anyone but himself and how this failure makes him immoral because the source of human morality is the ability to empathize and sympathize with others. Beyzaie also uses masks in a way that echoes (1) their use by ancient Iranian royalty to enhance their charisma and prevent people from seeing them as normal humans, and (2) their use in rituals for similar purposes and facilitating role play as in ta'ziyeh where masks range from full body animal masks to face coverings for actors playing the roles of male or female saints.

The play begins by Zahhâk waking up and engaging in a repartee with the two sisters in which the two women's relationship with Zahhâk is gradually revealed. Beyzaie's fast paced and multi-layered dialogue implies a timeworn relationship between Zahhâk and the two sisters and opens the plot in medias res, the night before the revolution that is to topple Zahhâk. In line with the concurrently realistic and surrealistic world of A Thousand Tales, Zahhâk's a thousand years' reign is said to have been one thousand days in which people's suffering was so intense that it felt like a thousand years. In line with the traditional Iranian idea of time, the sunset is the end of one and the beginning of the next 24-hour circle. Thus, the one thousand and first night occurs before the one thousand and first day which is the day of Zahhâk's downfall.

Evolving to reflect this night as a revolutionary moment, the plot initiates a conflict marked with carnival motifs that combine repartee with comic comments that subvert the hierarchy of power. This carnival begins as Arnavâz places an imaginary crown on her head to initiate the tale that reveals their conspiracy like the plot of a play about ending Zahhâk's reign. The dialogue also reveals Zahhâk's obsession with distributing pain and intimidation to maintain power and shows how the rock reliefs of ancient times functioned like modern propaganda. It also echoes Zahhâk's tale. Thus, "Ahriman's three moves" echo how the devil enticed him to commit patricide, returned later as a chef to make him obsessed with meaty foods and kiss his shoulders from which snakes grew, and finally appeared as a physician who prescribed two human brains to calm his snakes. Whereas Jamshid is associated with the sun, plants, trees, and prosperity, Zahhâk is associated with blind power, draught, famine, burning and massacre. He brags about the process that led to his rise to power and how his fear mongering techniques have engineered his conquests, but the sisters can only see how this Faustian process has undone his humanity.

The sisters also associate Fereydun with fertility by commenting on his rebuilding of irrigation and freshwater ducts and mark him as an initiating hero raised by a sacred cow, a man whose bullhead steel mace represents his defence of farmers and herdsmen against invading tyrants. Shahrnâz's dream also foreshadows Zahhâk's defeat and enchainment in Damavand Mount. Whereas Zahhâk destroys everything, Fereydun, the champion of life, is to chain the demon of draught and organize human and natural resources to create prosperity.

The dialogue also marks the sisters as bestowers of legitimacy, as kingmakers, a role that in the *Shahnameh* is usually preserved for leading heroes such as Rostam or Gīv. Beyzaie, thus, also comments on how the rise of the new woman in Iran's cultural arena has transformed the nature of power relations and may, indeed, produce positive outcomes if the new woman is not trapped by the contemporary forms of toxic femininity. This kingmaking role, however, also makes sense at the archetypal level in which they stand for the spirits of water and earth refusing to endorse the usurping demon of draught, and at the political level as they are the daughters of the ideal sun-king. However, before they start their performance of how they tricked Zahhâk, the play also uses the metaphor of people straightening their back to reiterate its point about how a just system that supports productivity releases people of the economic burdens that they have under exploiting tyrants so that they can metaphorically stand up and become real citizens rather than bow like serfs under the pressure of life.

Another trope in the sisters' performance is sacrificial leadership, reflected in Shahrnâz's willingness to ruin her reputation by volunteering to marry Zahhâk to buy his trust, initiate the one thousand days of kingship prophesized for him and find a way to reduce people's suffering until he can be toppled. While echoing Shahrzâd's function as a sacrificial trickster in *A Thousand Tales*, the plot also explains why popular or epic tales may neglect such sacrificial strategies which have historically played significant roles in the continuity of a culture. The play's ideal leader, therefore, is concerned with people's conditions and the continuity of the positive aspects of the culture rather than her own political or even historical reputation. For Zahhâk, the participating audience and the political opportunist, this is just stupid, but being beyond an unscrupulous desire for reputation or power, she only aspires to save people. The emphasis on sacrificial leadership also echoes the cultural conditions of the contemporary era in which the traditional practice of comparing bad monarchs with Zahhâk associated the extremists of the Islamic republic with Zahhâk because their violent power-obsessed policies and their fixation on suppressing cultural activities place them in the category that Beyzaie associates with the demons of draught in agricultural myths. The same analogy is applicable to the play on the Indian falconer and his lovely wife. The man's mean nature makes him unable to have a proper relationship with his creative and caring wife. Thus, he constantly tries to limit and punish her for imagined sins, an attitude that proves to be his greatest enemy as it alienates his wife and the chicks she has been caring for. The play also reflects this in the way the sisters try to reform Zahhâk by asking him to starve and slay his snakes, the emblems of his demonic misanthropy, so that people can approach and love him to initiate prosperity. Yet, being obsessed with revenge and power, Zahhâk fails to transcend his destructive attitudes towards people.

Beyzaie's handling of the theme of ideal leadership is done in a way that it also subverts the cliche of spoiled femininity. Thus, the sisters use the excuse of being fussy eaters to employ their former royal chefs who can assist them in their emancipatory mission. He also uses a similar technique to subvert the stereotype of women bending to the charm of powerful men regardless of their character. The sister trick Zahhak into believing they are charmed by his power, but in reality they are plotting to dethrone him. Unlike others who may be obsessed with their reputation, the two sisters do what is right regardless of its short- and long-term consequences for their reputation. Thus, in metaphors that associate them with the goddesses of earth and water protecting the people and preparing the path for the heroes of fertility, they save the 1001 men who fulfil the liberating revolution. The final dialogue, therefore, celebrates women as the unsung heroes of Iran's continuity.

Zahhâk: *[On his knees]* Your name will be erased! You are stupid! Heroes will come and chain me; and you will get naught but censure for being my wives! In the tales they tell about the battle, there will be no words about you; yes — in the victory that will come, no one will even remember you!

Shahrnâz: I did not do this for name, Zahhâk; neither did my sister Arnavâz. We are Jam's daughters; we adorn the world with justice and are cut into death with saws of injustice.

Thus, the injustice of cutting Jamshid, the initiator of Iranian civilization, into half is compared with the injustice of cutting women out of the history of the continuity of this civilization.[1] Thus, in the first part, Beyzaie, once more, fulfils his self-assigned mission of showing to his audience what they are not used to seeing and writing a history of unseen people.[2]

Part Two: The Creative Intellectuals as Sacrificial Heroes

Beyzaie's focus on the history of unseen people evolves in the second part to include a history of an unseen book and the atrocities imposed on Iranians during the early centuries after Islam, which were rationalized later as the country's conversion to Islam meant that the promoters of the dominant discourse associated any discussion of such atrocities with heresy. Once more, this has a contemporary significance as the play's events echo those of the post-revolution era and such scandals as the widespread interrogations, tortures, and executions of the people in the 1980s or the chain murders of the 1990s in which dissenting intellectuals

---

1. For a more detailed analysis of the first part, see Talajooy, "Reformulation", 710-19.
2. See Beyzaie in Omid, *Târikh*, 749 and Dabashi, *Close-up*, 84.

and artists were targeted by groups that were later found to be the secret operatives of intelligence offices.

Thus, the idea of a usurping centre destroying intellectual productivity by sequestrating its products to fulfil its distorted desires and ruining the lives of their producers is as relevant to contemporary Iran as the early Islamic era or any other era branded by a usurping centre. As his *Journalistic World of Mr Asrâri* (1966) or *Account of Bondar the Premier* (1960) suggests, this idea has been important to Beyzaie since a young age. However, with the 1980s bringing him face to face with a clique of state officials who fired him from his university job and did not allow him to make films but used his ideas and technical innovations or even his filmscripts, as in *The Fateful Day* (1995) to promote their own discourses, his old experiences of living in a Kafkaesque world of inexplicable and grotesque punishments resurfaced.

Nevertheless, the re-enactment of the torture scene in the style of a *ta'ziyeh* play and the plays' multi-layered suggestiveness transcend this political level to mark the atrocities that have historically distorted life in Iran and signify how, as Beyzaie also illustrated in *Ballad of Tara* (1978), rather than Hossein and his family, the real victims of the atrocities committed in the early centuries of Islam and afterwards were Iranians and the other victims of the conquests that hid themselves behind a religion. In this case, the three protagonists, like millions of others who suffered similar fates, are Muslims, but this does not save them from the greed of the racist elites who use religion to rob them of whatever they have including their lives.

Once more, the play begins in media res, after the protagonists' residence in Baghdad for one thousand days. Beyzaie begins the exposition with an apparently mild yet portentous ambiance in which the dialogue, background, mise en scene and finally the *ta'ziyeh*-like re-enactment of Pour-e Farrokhân's death build the tension to suggest the crushing surveillance and suffocation that one may suffer under a tyrannical regime that justifies its atrocities with religion.

The first turning point in this process occurs when this implied anxiety is actualized by the Sheriff of Baghdad's destruction of *A Thousand Tales* by putting it in a bucket of water. As in Beyzaie's other works, the scene echoes actual events. In his *Biographies of*

Poets (ca. 1491), after referring to a pre-Islamic poem on the dedication tablet on the gate of Shirin's Palace which "had still survived until the time of Azud al-Dawla Deilami [r. 949 to 983]" Dolatshah Samarqandi argues that since in the first two centuries after Islam, Arab rulers endeavoured to supplant Persian traditions, it is likely that they also forbade recording poetry in Persian and that the change of script made it impossible to continue its tradition. He, then, continues:

> Abdollah Ibn-e Taher [R. 828-844] was the governor of Khorasan in the Abbasid era. One day a man brought him a book as a gift. He asked: "What book is this?" The man said: "This is the story of *Vâmeq and Azrâ*. It is a great story that men of knowledge compiled for Khosrow I [R. 531-79]. The governor said: "We and our people read nothing but the Quran and the prophet's sayings. We don't need such books. This was written by the Magi and is unacceptable to us. Then, he ordered the book to be thrown into the water and issued a decree requiring that all the books compiled or authored by Iranians or the Magi be burned in his realm.[1]

A similar case involving the massacre of men of knowledge and destruction of books can be found in Biruni's reports of how in 712 Qotaybat Ibn-e Muslim (669-715) killed everyone who read Khwarizmi or knew the history of the region.[2] Though this was not representative of all Arab rulers and some reports indicate that some were supportive of scholars,[3] the play is not concerned with destroying books or suppressing learning. It is rather concerned with an ethnocentric form of appropriation that originates in inferiority complex and is bent on destroying the evidence of the cultural superiority of a conquered people.

This historical embedding and the presence of three intellectuals allow Beyzaie to focus on the possibility of familial or social fulfilment under religious tyranny. In this context, Mâhak's suggestions about how they worry about each other and *Hezâr Afsân*, a token of the beauty of their culture, evolves into Pour-e

---

1. Samarqandi, *Tazkerat*, 26.
2. Biruni, *Al-Âthâr*, 57-8. (English, 42).
3. See Motahari's Islamically biased *Khadamât*, 307-21, which, still, contains some correct references.

Farrakhan's justification of the book's content by comparing his torturers with the demons who do whatever they like to people or his comparing of Zahhâk's devouring of brains with how tyrants kill the people of knowledge, take the products of their brains and distort those ideas to feed their tyranny! The protagonists' role as sacrificial intellectuals who speak truth to power is also placed along nightmarish and Kafkaesque motifs that reflect the simplicity of people's expectations and family relations and the grotesque reality of living under the surveillance, violence, and sexual or power obsessions of corrupt rulers.

With the arrival of the Iranian, who has "written everything" down, the anxiety of being unable to control one's life in such a society is sublimated as the three undergo stylized metamorphosis to become actors in a passion play that commemorate a sacrificial hero. Beyzaie directly refers to Manichean passion rituals and echoes the biographies of such mystic martyrs of knowledge as Mansur-e Al-Hallaj (858-922), Eyn-al-Qozat Hamedani (1098–1131) and Shahabeddin Sohrevardi (1155–1192), and many others who were brutally tortured and destroyed along their books by Iranian, Arab or Turkic "defenders of true religion".[1] Yet, his approach also echoes the large scale historical wiping of knowledge and people exemplified in such events as Sultan Mahmud's invasion of Rey, which the writer of *Mojmal* justifies in religious terms: "He had nooses set up and hanged the elites of Daylam on trees and had some sewen in bull's skin and sent to Ghazni. He took fifty Kharvârs (15 tons) of Shi'i, Ismaili and philosophy books out of their houses and had them burnt under the trees on which they had been hanged."[2]

The focus on Pour-e Farrokhân's torture, therefore, highlights how obsession with religion or authority has historically allowed greed and sadism to be justified in religious or political terms and how violence has derailed cultural reform in Iranian history. Similarly, the ritual killing of Pour-e Farrokhân by having scribes break their inkbottles on his head also reflects the traditional method of having people with the same job as the condemned

---

1. For more on religious suppression, see Nezâm-ol-Molk, *Siyâsatnâmeh*, chapters 44-47.
2. Bahar (Ed.), *Mojmal*, 311-2.

person denounce him by acting as his executioners.[1] The same idea, however, also signifies how in tyrannical systems petty rivalries, fear or sycophancy may turn normal people into executioners.

Beyzaie emphasizes this point by having Mâhak list the atrocious types of state and religious violence recorded in history: "Did they break his bones? Did blood spurt out of his throat? Did they cut out his eyes? Did they smash his fingers?" The emphasis on political and religious violence can be further analysed in light of Pierre Bourdieu's arguments about state violence: "the state is an X […] which successfully claims the monopoly of the legitimate use of physical and symbolic violence over a definite territory and over the totality of the corresponding population".[2] The problem with this monopoly, however, is that while rationalized in terms of upholding order, it always transgresses its own standards in ways that are hard to control as it is often exerted by unscrupulous agents or rulers on those with no power in the system.

This motif also reflects the way intelligence organizations justify their own budgets by torturing people to obtain weird confessions that help them present any sociopolitical protest in society or art as a conspiracy headed by foreigners. This is best revealed in the Prosecutor's statement: "You will be free only when you give us the details of this conspiracy, so we know if you, damned wretch, are alone in this plot or a group of Iranians are with you in this!" This is also the case when he reduces *A Thousand Tales* into a political allegory against the Arabs. Thus, when Poure Farrokhân states that the myth of Zahhâk "is a tale of the age of epic, and *A Thousand Tale* belongs to the age of reason in which the sword is of no use!" he responds, "is this not but a nation under the blade of the executioner looking for a way to save itself?" *A Thousand Tales*, like Beyzaie's play, inspires resistance against toxic politics, but the torturers reduce it to their own case as they know that they are also on the evil side of the relations of power.

---

1. For an example, see Tabari, *Târikh*, vol. 2, 702-3, the account of Khosrow I, having one of his scribes who had dared question his new taxing policy killed in the same manner.
2. Bourdieu, *Practical*, 40.

These motifs are embedded in a *ta'ziyeh* template which augments their significance by suggesting that the template has been created by Iranians to condemn victimization of positive aspects of culture. As in *ta'ziyeh*, in which the actual identities of amateur actors negated their performance because they wanted to distance themselves from the evil characters they played or they were really upset about what was happening to the protagonists, Khurzâd and Mâhak bewail Pour-e Farrokhân while playing his torturers. The Iranian also acts like a *ta'ziyeh* director by reminding them of how they must play their roles. *Ta'ziyeh* elements can also be seen in the recurrent use of religious term to highlight how religion is manipulated to justify grotesque violence. Thus, Pour-e Farrokhân frequently quotes the Quranic phrase, "In the Name of God the Compassionate the Merciful", but his torturers respond by words that suggest God is revengeful, and while the book is to become a source of pleasure for the Caliph, "the successor of the prophet" its translator is being executed for attempting to ruin the religion.

Ta'ziyeh elements are also reflected in that rather than focusing on performance for survival in an epic (male-centred) or a folktale (female-centred) mode, the ritual enables the two to identify with the sacrificial heroes to be able to liberate themselves through death from sexual bondage. Thus, like Sadeq Hedayat's Parvin in *Parvin the Daughter of Sassan* (1928), they prefer to die rather than survive as sexual slaves of the tyrants that have killed their families and dreams. The double stabbing, however, suggests the archetypal idea of the sun's descendent (Khurzâd) and the moon's crescent (Mâhak), the sources of boding enlightenment, initiating their own eclipse and the temporary eclipse of Iranian culture to avoid serving the grotesque form of tyranny that they observe around them.

As in Beyzaie's *Death of Yazdegerd*, the re-enactment of the torture/court scene also function to turn the judges into the judged. The whole religiously tyrannical systems of Omayyad and Abbasid Caliphates and their later Iranian or non-Iranian predecessors and successors are, thus, put on trial. It also allows the main characters to play multiple roles which suggest how performance enables us to understand the mentality of the other in its positive or negative senses. Originally, it seems as if the plot was set by the Sheriff of

Baghdad to endear himself with the Caliph yet avoid paying the money he has promised to Pour-e Farrokhân, but it soon becomes clear that the Caliph himself provided the guidelines for appropriating the masterpiece, removing its Iranian signs and destroying the original to manufacture evidence for proving the superiority of his culture.

Another motif in the second play focuses on how the obsession of the ruling elites to rename people and places to wipe out their history and identity disrupts cultural continuity. This is first introduced in the way the Sheriff translates the protagonists' names into Arabic to disrupt their Iranian identity. It, then, evolves to mark the way the name, characters, history and locations of the book were distorted so that *A Thousand Tales* became *One Thousand and One Nights* in Arabic and ended up as *Arabian Nights* in English. Beyzaie directly refers to this point when the Caliph issues a decree requiring that his agents "wash the book of its Iranian signs, remove all the Magi customs, change the tales from the past to the present, and from Ctesiphon to Baghdad, and burn the original!" Thus, though the chronology of Shahryar as a Sasanian king (224-652) signifies the fallacy of Shahrzâd telling tales about Harun al-Rashid's court (766-809), the only element that remained Iranian was the framing story, which probably remined unchanged because the new rulers thought that it would be better if the evil Shahryar, Shahryar's and Shahzamân's promiscuous wives, and the trickster Shahrzâd and Dinâzâd remain Iranian.

The concern with the identity of Iranians is also evident in Beyzaie's use of language in the second part which is overwhelmed by Arabic loanwords. While displaying Beyzaie's unique mastery in reformulating different class registers of Persian from various historical eras, this use of language and the protagonists' concern about the language also suggests how a language may lose its normal texture, beauty and communication potential due to colonial impositions rather than normal intercultural borrowings. Thus, Beyzaie's concern is a reflection on how New Persian which evolved with a natural flow of intercultural cross-fertilization with about 10% Arabic loanwords mostly in religious and trade contexts reached a situation in which official correspondences were so intensely Arabized and ornate by the 1600s that normal Iranians who did not know Arabic hardly understood their content.

The second part, thus, closes in a bleak ambiance with the physical deaths or the self-imposed setting of the budding moon and sun, but the audacity of the two women's action reflect the possibility that the existence of such women and men may trigger a later rebirth of the culture.

Part Three: Rebirth of the Light

While occurring centuries later, the third part of the play begins with another death ritual in which Roshanak, a woman of about 21, and her sister, Rokhsân, a girl of about 15, are preparing for a performance in which Roshanak is to fake her death. The dialogue reveals that Roshanak has been creating a Shahrzâd-like plan to reform Mir Khân, her present husband, ever since she saw him as the head of a group of young men who were to close her mother's girl's school at the behest of their town's clergies. It also specifies that her mother's self-immolation in reaction to the clerics' decree left an indelible mark on the minds of everyone involved.

The opening, therefore, makes a metaphoric reference to Khurzâd and Mâhak's suicides. Thus, their deaths, as Roshanak and Rokhsân's metaphoric mothers and former selves, are reframed for a rebirth in which rather than being wanted for their sexual appeal, they are respected for their intellectual abilities. Their engagement in a conspirative performance is also an echo of Shahrnâz and Arnavâz's epic and folk functions. Rather than launching a revolution, however, the intention here is reforming a man who may be capable of change if they can overcome his ignorance. Roshanak's metaphoric death, therefore, poses three questions about: (1) will their bravery, intellectual agency, and sacrifice remain masked like Shahrnâz and Arnavâz and they will be treated as if absent, (2) will they have to undergo philosophical suicide and become sexual objects or undergo actual suicide to avoid such a destiny, (3) or will they manage to reconstruct their fate and the fates of other women and men by reforming a man who is a role model for other man and can, thus, end the vicious circle of toxic masculinity?

The ritual ambiance of moving between death and rebirth is also enriched by ritual objects echoing the lives of women and the interior quarters of Iranian households. Thus, the initial references to object, professions and rituals associated with funerals make the merry ending more striking, particularly because the ending contains the promise of a child, the reopening of the school, a healthier relationship between Mir Khân and Roshanak, and a better future for Rokhsân and everyone else. The ritual aspect is also present in Beyzaie's use of symbolic names. Thus, Roshanak's name suggests enlightened, Rokhsân's being honest and beautiful and Mir Khân's an authority that can be put in service of construction or destruction.

Beyzaie, thus, examines the possibility of using creativity and open-minded knowledge to tame power for productivity rather than letting it remain obsessed with boosting itself with violence and outdated constructs. These outdated constructs which enter the minds before individuals are capable of thought are represented as the so-called "learned", the conveyors of inherited dogma, whose shadows continue to dominate Mir Khân's life. The system, however, has already received a heavy blow by a woman's launching of a school for girls and her self-immolation in face of the decree of closing it. Beyzaie suggests that such decrees are not much different from the one that prescribed two young brains for Zahhâk's snakes or had Pour-e Farrokhân killed and Khurzâd and Mâhak given as sex objects to his murderers. In other words, he equates the decree of Iblis in Zahhâk's myth with the decree of the Caliph and his clergy in the eighth century and that of the learned men or the clergy of the first decade of the twentieth century. The mother, however, delivered two blows to the system. The first was to bring smiling young girls dreaming of better futures to the public space in a school that functioned better than the one run by the clergy. The second was to subvert the norms of social performance by sacrificing her life for a new beginning. Both acts have sown the seeds for changing what Jacques Rancière calls "the distribution of the sensible", the range of activities, voices and perspectives that are allowed to be seen and heard in society without being condemned as anti-social or anti-religion noises or deeds that must be brutally suppressed. [1] The emphasis on the children's bodies, laughter, and learning and their teacher's later self-immolation as a protest against the suffocating ambiance of her culture highlights how her deeds transgressed the suppressive aesthetics at the core of the system that decided what could be given the chance to present "itself to the senses" and become "visible" in the public space. Their mother, has, thus, burned like a source of light to transform the public space and the habitual ways of being.

Once more, Beyzaie condenses and heightens his subject to transcend the mundane and reflect the essential realities of living under exclusionist systems. Thus, Roshanak's mother is like the first women who campaigned for women's education in Iran, particularly Bibi Khanum Astarabadi (1858-1921), the writer of the first feminist pamphlet in Iran *Ma'âyeb al-Rejâl* (Vices of Men, 1894), whose newly opened, home-based *Dabestân-e Dushizegân* (School for Girls) which was also attended by the mothers and grandmothers of the girls who studied there, was damaged by a fire set by the thugs working for a dogmatic clergy in 1907. [2]

What Roshanak and Rokhsân do, therefore, is to complete a Shahrâzâd-like ideal for which their mother scarified her life in a plot that links the history of women's liberation with that of the translation of *One Thousand and One Night* into Persian (1844) and the clerics' suppression of a book in which a woman acts as a saviour. Thus, Beyzaie's play moves from epic and folktale recitation to sacrificial tragedy and ends with a comedy of manners in which Rokhsân functions like, Black, the clever sidekick of Iranian improvisatory comedies. This comedy evolves with a dramatic irony in which Rokhsân, and the audience know that Roshanak is okay, but Mir Khân does not. In Iranian comedies, such situations are used to poke fun at the ignorance of a figure of authority through a clever servant who may also be involved in

---

1. Rancière, *Politics*, 13.
2. Despite the clergy's accusations and challenges, Bibi Khanum's school, in which her two daughters also taught, continued to educate girls. Another woman involved in founding girls' schools was Tuba Roshdiyeh, aka Tuba Azmudeh (1878-1936) who faced similar challenges. See also Najmabadi, *Women*, 181-206.

helping a young couple to fulfil their love for each other, which, in turn, offers the promise of fertility. In Beyzaie's play, the figure of authority himself is liberated from his ignorance to become the young hero, and Rokhsân functions like the clever servant who ridicules both her sister and Mir Khân while helping her sister to fulfil her plan for reforming or leaving him.

Besides making sarcastic remarks or interrupting his master by speaking, laughing or crying, the clever servant of Iranian comedies usually uses the following methods to provoke laughter. In *pakari* (pensive deflation) he "engages his victims in serious discussions" only to ridicule their reactions in the end. In *Navâ dar âvardan* (copying the voice) he duplicates a person's accent, tone, or common word choices to display their inanity. In *Hamdardi* (sympathy) he pretends to have sympathy for a person or joins them to do something stupid only to prove them stupid. In *tahammoq* (fooling) he "pretends to be stupid" to be able to insult wealthy or influential people. In *taqlib* (twisting), he ridicules his boss by malapropism, repeating the name of an object or food they loathe to disarm them, approvingly comparing them to beasts, flattering them for qualities they lack, turning their exclamations of "pain or anger into funny songs," or interrupting their "serious speech by crying or laughing noisily".[1]

Rokhsân's teasing remarks work with these techniques to suggest her individuality and desire for fulfilment. Whereas Roshanak is more of an intellectual planner and writer, Rokhsân is more of a witty artist and improvisor capable of extracting joy from the heart of sadness. Rokhsân's desire for fulfilment also allows the repartee between them to comment on ideals of manhood and womanhood, on gender as performance and on how this performance can be detrimental to family relationships and cultural, socio-political and scientific progress if it is trapped in restrictive constructs imposed by religious or political dogma. The play shows how this performance can be flexible to let men and woman use their power and energy to serve their family in its path to prosperity and mutual fulfilment and how dependence on outdated constructs and relations leads to a situation in which the man and the woman try to suppress and control each other and their

---

1. Talajooy, "Indigenous," 516.

157

children. It also comments on how patriarchal constructs keep the world of men and women so apart that mutual understanding rarely occurs, and neutral qualities that have nothing to do with gender may be praised in one and condemned in the other. As Roshanak puts it in a dialogue which is also relevant to Shahrzâd's achievement as a champion of wisdom, "Wisdom is called cunning when it comes to women! And cunning is called reason when it comes to men!".

Another key motif in the third part is Roshanak's avoidance of violence. Like her mother, the fire she has in her is not the fire of hate or love but one of light which is to enlighten the future by transforming an embodiment of hegemonic masculinity into an agent of progress. Thus, rather than planning to revenge by killing those who caused her parent's deaths, she takes her revenge against the discourse that has produced such people. She even pities them and knowing that they have been deceived to assume that this discourse provides them with the best of both worlds, she aspires to change them by reforming their role model.

Conclusion and Reception

The third play, therefore, completes Beyzaie's reflections on the unseen agency of women by focusing on how women can be instrumental in subverting the suppressive constructs of inherited patriarchy, the remaining vestiges of the toxic relations that produced people of Zahhâk's type and became sacrosanct with religion. The play, thus, closes with the suggestion that openness to knowledge, creativity and mutual support and engaging in constructive action for creating an egalitarian culture may be the path forward. This, however, does not mean Roshanak and Rokhsân's dominance. It rather means a rebirth for both men and women. Once more, Roshanak clearly expresses this with: "[To Mir Khân.] And why shouldn't it be your rebirth? Give me the key to the school building. My mother is there under a stone, sleeping in her ashes. Let's go and light up her light; with the same fire in which she burned!"

Beyzaie himself staged the play from 16 September 2003 to 7 November 2003 in Tehran to high acclaim. The reviews written at the time were divided. Almost everyone praised Beyzaie's mastery in reformulating Iranian dramatic idioms and his use of language. A few, however, took the second play out of context and instead of realizing that Beyzaie is concerned with the impacts of colonization on a culture, the violent nature of tyranny and the contemporary suppression of cultural activities criticized Beyzaie for setting the lines of evil and good along the ethnic lines of Arabs and Iranians and showing signs of radical nationalism.[1] Rather than being nationalistic, however, Beyzaie aptly depicts the nature of religious tyranny by historical distancing, and this is also highlighted in the fact that Zahhâk's father, a just Arab ruler, is his first victim. At the political level, therefore, rather than being nationalistic, Beyzaie is concerned with highlighting the impacts of such forms of domination on people and culture and showing how a book like *One Thousand and One Night* confronts such forms of tyranny by empowering women while deconstructing the post-revolutionary discourses that obsessively promoted the Islamic side of Iranian identity at the expense of other aspects.

Since its publication, the play has been repeatedly staged and has continued to be a touchstone of Shakespearean qualities for actors and directors. During the last decade, Mojdeh Shamsaie has also used her powerful presence on the stage and her unique performing skills in several solo performances of the first part of the play in which she successfully played the role of the ten characters that appear in the first part. In 2017, when Beyzaie came to the University of St Andrews to receive his honorary doctorate, I had the honour of organizing and seeing her performance which has left an indelible mark on my memory due to its captivating intensity and her ability to step in and out of each role with so much precision and grace.

---

[1] See, for instance, Rezaei-Rad, "Goftârhâei," 28.

Bibliography

Bahar, Mohammad Taqi. Ed. *Mojmal al-Tavarikh va al-Qessas*. Unknown writer 1128. Tehran: Khâvar, 1939.

------------. *The Chronology of Ancient Nations; an English Version of the Arabic Text of the Athâr-ul-Bâkiya of Albîrûnî, or "Vestiges of the Past"*. Translated by Eduard Sachau. London: Oriental translation Fund, 1879.

Beyzaie, Bahram. *Riysheh-Yâbi-ye Derakht-e Khoan*. Tehran: Roshangarân, 2004

-----------. *Hezâr Afsân Kojâst?* TehranL Roshangarân, 2012.

-----------. 'Ostureh-hā dar Āsār-e Bahram Beyzaie.' Video Recording. Available at Aparat.com. <shorturl.at/bjsCY> (Last accessed on 17/12/2021).

Bourdieu, Pierre. *Practical Reason: On the Theory of Action*. Cambridge: Polity Press, 1998.

Dabashi, Hamid. *Close Up: Iranian Cinema, Past, Present, and Future*. London: Verso, 2001.

Ibn-e Nadim, *The Fihrist of al-Nadim: A Tenth Century Survey of Muslim Culture*, Vol. 2. (986 AD). Ed. and Trans. Bayard Dodge. New York: Columbia UP, 1970.

Mas'udi, Ali. "Chapter 68". *Moravvej al-Zahab va Ma'aden al-Johar* (947 AD), Persian trans. Abolqasem Payandeh. Tehran: Elmi va Farhangi, (1965), 2003.

Motahari, Morteza. *Khadamât-e Moteqâbel Iran va Islam*. Tehran: Nasimemotahar.com, 2021.

Najmabadi, Afsaneh. *Women with Moustaches and Men without Beards: Gender and Sexual Anxieties of Iranian Modernity*. Berkeley: University of California Press, 2005.

Nizam al-Mulk. *The Book of Government or Rules for Kings: The Siyar al-Muluk or Siyasat-nama of Nizam al-Mulk.* Translated by Hubert Darke. New York and London: Routledge, 1960.

Omid, Jamal. *Târikh-e Cinema-ye Iran 1279-1357.* Tehran: Rozaneh, 1374/1995.

Rancière, Jacques. *The Politics of Aesthetics: The Distribution of the Sensible.* Trans. Gabriel Rockhill. London: Continuum, 2004.

Rezaei-Rad, Mohamad. "Goftârhâei Âdami-Shekl" *Honarhâ-ye Namâyeshi* (Oct. 2003), 27-9.

Samarqandi, Dolatshah-e *Tazkerat-o-Shoara.* Edited. Mohamad Ramezani. Tehran: Padideh Khâvar, 1987.

Talajooy, Saeed. "Indigenous Performing Traditions in Post-Revolutionary Iranian Theatre," Iranian Studies, 44, no. 4, (July 2011), 497-519.

----------. "Reformulation of Shahnameh Legends in Bahram Beyzaie's Plays." *Iranian Studies.* Vol. 46, no. 5 (Autumn 2013), 695-719.

-----------. "Intellectuals as Sacrificial Heroes: A Comparative Study of Bahram Beyzaie and Wole Soyinka." *Comparative Literature Studies.* Vol. 52, no. 2 (2015), 379-408.

-----------. "History and Iranian Drama: The Case of Bahram Beyzaie". In *Perceptions of Iran: History, Myths and Nationalism from Medieval Persia to the Islamic Republic.* Ed. Ali Ansari. London: Bloomsbury, 2013. 183-209.

Yarshater, Ehsan. "AFRÂSÎÂB". Encyclopaedia Iranica Online, © Trustees of Columbia University in the City of New York. Consulted online on 13 February 2021
<http://dx.doi.org/10.1163/2330-4804_EIRO_COM_4841>

www.ingramcontent.com/pod-product-compliance
Lightning Source LLC
Chambersburg PA
CBHW011040190726
48290CB00011B/2942